Keith Parks
Breaking Barriers & Opening Frontiers

Gary Baldridge

Keith Parks
Breaking Barriers & Opening Frontiers

Gary Baldridge

SMYTH&HELWYS
PUBLISHING. INCORPORATED   MACON. GEORGIA
WWW.HELWYS.COM

SMYTH&
HELWYS

Smyth & Helwys Publishing, Inc.
6316 Peake Road
Macon, Georgia 31210-3960
1-800-747-3016
©1999 by Smyth & Helwys Publishing

Gary Baldridge

Library of Congress Cataloging-in-Publication Data

Baldridge, Gary.
        Keith Parks: breaking barriers and opening frontiers.
        1. Parks, R. Keith.
        2. Southern Baptist Convention Biography.
        3. Cooperative Baptist Fellowship Biography.
        4. Baptists—United States Biography.
        5. Missionaries—United States Biography.
        I. Title.
        BX6495.P278B35   1999
        266'.61'092—dc21   99-14808
        [B]   CIP

ISBN 1-57312-286-6

Contents

My goal was to share the Good News, not where they already had access, that I might not simply add to another person's initial work, but as the prophet said, "Those who had no word of him will see, those who hadn't heard will take it to heart."

—Romans 15:20-21
author's paraphrase

Preface

When Keith Parks first learned of plans for this book, he responded with a grin, "I guess I'll have to start watching what I say around you!"

It was too late. From my first day with the Cooperative Baptist Fellowship (CBF), 13 May 1996, I had the good fortune to occupy an office near one of America's finest missionary leaders. After awhile I started taking notes when he spoke in administrative team meetings, around a lunch table, in the hallways, and to missionary candidates, new missionaries, missionaries on leave, missionaries at conferences, and missionaries in team meetings. I collected his brief reports, copies of correspondence, and other documents.

As a former missionary to regions other than those he frequented, I was struck by the similarities of experiences and by how much his own philosophy of missions had influenced thousands of missionaries, including me. His stories were delightful, his sense of humor a breath of fresh air in a field of work that can often come across as too Spartan or too rigid.

The best part of all was working for Keith Parks. In reality, it was more a case of working "with" instead of "for." He gave a lot of latitude to his staff and kept control of nothing but the big picture, the overarching concepts guiding daily work. His principles were the only unchanging aspect of his ministry, and he guarded those jealously. While his critics saw him as stubborn and too single-minded, those who worked with him understood his reasons for the few unbending positions he took and realized his vision drove him.

There will never be another like Keith Parks. He represented some of the best qualities of a particular, Texas Baptist tradition and worked in such a way that his accomplishments might give glory to God alone.

While the learning curve for this book stretched over my two decades in Baptist missions, and while the notes piled up over two years, I wrote this book during the evenings and weekends in a seven-week period marked by an unusual number of trips and conferences. These included a six-day, round-the-world journey and a week's worth of meetings in the Midwest and on the East Coast. As a result, this book simply highlights the principal contributions of Keith Parks at his retirement. I leave the task of producing a definitive study to Baptist historians in the new millennium.

Acknowledgments

To Keith Parks I owe much, here specifically for his willingness to clarify points throughout the book and to suggest several additional sources. Helen Jean Parks gave invaluable advice, too.

Thanks also to the home staff and field staff of Cooperative Baptist Fellowship, Atlanta, Georgia; to some at the Southern Baptist Convention's International Mission Board, Richmond, Virginia; and to former missionaries for their perspectives, especially Alan Neely, Bill O'Brien, and Harlan Spurgeon. The feature stories of CBF journalist Robert O'Brien also helped greatly, along with his work in securing a loan of the Foreign Mission Board (now the International Mission Board) photographs.

The one book of most help to me was William R. Estep's *Whole Gospel, Whole World: The Foreign Mission Board of the Southern Baptist Convention, 1845-1995.* I'm also grateful for a look at Parks' first-draft copy of some of the transcripts of his oral history memoir, taped in October 1997 during interviews by Bill Pitts of the Baylor University Institute for Oral History, Waco, Texas.

Finally, my wife, Barbara, provided great counsel for the various drafts of text, straight from her own missionary heart.

Chronology

23 October 1927	Born in Memphis, Texas
24 May 1952	Married Helen Jean Bond of Abilene, Texas
April 1954	Appointed by the Foreign Mission Board to Indonesia
1968–1975	Area Secretary, Southeast Asia
1975–1979	Director, Mission Support Division, Foreign Mission Board
1980–1992	President, Foreign Mission Board
1993–1999	Global Missions Coordinator, Cooperative Baptist Fellowship
28 February 1999	Retired after 45 years in global missions

Chapter 1

Pushing to the Frontier of Missions

*The most important acts, both for the one who accomplishes
them and for his fellow creatures, are those that have remote
consequences.*

—Leo Tolstoy

On the sparsely populated Syrian-Iraqi border, far from
modern Damascus and seventy-five miles east of the Syrian
town of Qamishli, a grandfatherly figure climbed aboard a
small motorboat. He looked out across an arid, rolling ter-
rain on a beautiful clear day in June 1996, five years after the
Gulf War. The man's Kurdish escort steered the boat across
the Tigris River at a point used by smugglers. The tiny vessel
kept slipping sideways and fighting upstream on the swift
current. Finally the boat landed on the far bank, in Kurdish-
held, northern Iraq.

The American then joined grateful Cooperative Baptist
Fellowship (CBF) representatives, who were inspired and
encouraged by the visit amid rumors of an imminent thrust
northward by Saddam Hussein. The Muslim escorts, special
bodyguards of a Kurdish faction who carried multiple pass-
ports and identities, had no way of knowing the solitary
stranger, Dr. R. Keith Parks, had contributed as much to the
gospel's penetration into so-called "closed" countries as any
missions leader in the twentieth century.

That fact remains little known even among most
missions-minded Christians. Although his name is easily
recognized by many longtime Southern Baptists, Parks
receives little notice for his indisputable role in the shaping
of contemporary pioneer missions. Without his direct
empowerment of Baptists in frontier missions, more than

200 million non-Christians in Asia and elsewhere would have significantly fewer opportunities to hear the gospel today. Overcoming institutional resistance and even some missionary opposition, he championed a bold new approach for Southern Baptists to pioneer fields that revolutionized the success rate for penetrating vast numbers of ethnic homelands where traditional missionaries were not welcomed. For the first time in Christian history, no tribe or ethnic group in the world was absolutely beyond the potential reach of the gospel.

This man with a wry, Texas-sized wit, "having more fun than was legal," saw the future of frontier missions and implemented the strategy that would open some regions to the gospel for the first time. Because of Parks' leadership in the two closing decades of the twentieth century, Baptists in the South have had far more impact on the least-evangelized peoples of the world today. Moreover, the larger Christian missions community has had far more trained personnel and more resources to help fulfill the Great Commission of Jesus Christ (Matt 28:18-20).

"He has been on the cutting edge of world evangelization," CBF Coordinator Daniel Vestal wrote 1 October 1998, to CBF leaders, staff, and missionaries after Parks announced his retirement would come on 28 February 1999. "The influence of CBF in the world mission enterprise is important, far beyond our size and years. We're already a significant participant and influence in global missions, and I see no reason why that influence will not grow.

"What has happened in the past six years under Keith's leadership is cause for all of us to rejoice," Vestal noted. "A missions strategy that is distinctive and attractive has been clearly articulated, and the result is that Baptist churches and individuals are committed and involved."

Those six CBF years, combined with the last six years (1986-1992) of his twelve-year tenure as president of the Southern Baptist Foreign Mission Board (FMB) had a tremendous impact on the astonishing numbers of minorities and others overseas who started hearing the gospel for the first time. By late 1992 when he left the FMB, approximately 100 large ethnic or tribal "nations," people groups, with a combined population totaling hundreds of millions, were receiving unprecedented, full-time attention. This new care came from thousands of advocates, mobilizers, and church planters, from Baptists and from other denominations encouraged to cooperate in the campaign. These new missionaries to the formerly "closed" regions within Asia and North Africa seemed as mere drops in the ocean of need, but they were the first spray of many mounting waves to come.

It started in the early 1980s. Bill O'Brien, FMB executive vice president, received a nine-page, single-spaced letter from a Dr. David Barrett. An Anglican missionary and author of the mammoth *World Christian Encyclopedia,* Barrett shared his need to team up with an organization such as the FMB. That agency possessed sufficient resources for the development of a huge database and a missionary force capable of redeployment to large numbers of unevangelized fields. In 1983 Barrett was hired as a consultant to the FMB to help provide the data required for a new approach to peoples still awaiting the gospel. Focusing primarily on ethnolinguistic designations for population segments, for example, rather than the traditional approach by countries, Barrett and his assistants identified the tribes and ethnic groups having the least exposure to the gospel and proposed strategies to overcome the centuries-old barriers. The criteria used were indicators such as access to Christian shortwave broadcasts, Scripture translations,

Christians living in the vicinity, or just about any Christian influence whatsoever, however nominal it might seem.

Parks provided the power and influence needed to push these strategies beyond the objections of some of the FMB's administrators. Because of his support, the innovations saw the light of day starting in 1986 and flourishing the remainder of the century. Some traditional administrators vehemently opposed the concept from the beginning and would have killed or reconfigured the program at any stage along the way. They felt the nonresidential aspect threatened the incarnational ministry, referring to missionaries living long-term among the people, modeling the Christian life and message as Jesus did. They really did not understand how it could possibly work. Few of them had experience with secular-looking ministry designed to win approval for visas. These new paradigms required new vehicles (modern "wineskins") or "platforms," including creation of non-religious organizations on the field, rather than the old model of missions in which the Baptist sign was posted for all to see.

Others, for example, Ralph Winter, founder of the U.S. Center for World Mission, Pasadena, California, had proposed the people-group approach before Parks. Those in the Pasadena-Colorado Springs-Wheaton crowd saw the need as clearly as he did. The differences, however, were that Parks had in Barrett the new practical concept and the database, and in the FMB the financial and human resources necessary for a massive shift toward the most neglected peoples on earth. Most important of all, Parks championed the strategy that would open the doors through which many Great Commission people could walk.

Parks and his team were aided by the "coming of age" of computer technology, the 1989 collapse of the Soviet Union, the receptiveness of China, and the global economy's health.

The strategy was exciting in and of itself. Missionaries were trained in multiple roles while focusing on a specific people group (such as the Kurds), whose homeland might stretch across several international borders. These ambassadors for Christ worked in the roles of advocate, organizer, facilitator, liaison, promoter, recruiter, fund-raiser, and coach. Their purpose was to see that by all good means a particular people group would hear the Good News of Jesus Christ in this generation, ultimately through the multiple births of indigenous, reproducing congregations.

Parks opened up the strategy for use by other denominations and mission agencies. He agreed that his staff would train future trainers of any Christian organization willing to adopt the approach. Episcopalians, Pentecostals, and others took him up on the offer.

One of the crucial advantages Parks saw in the approach was its free engagement of Christians of all stripes, not just Baptists. The missionaries in the new program were encouraged to cooperate with any Christian denomination, any nationality, any parachurch organization wishing to partner with these Baptists on the frontiers. This new type of missionary was to call on the worldwide church, the entire body of Christ, to consider bringing some of its resources to bear upon the needs of a neglected people.

Intercessory prayer networks were linked around the globe. Round-the-clock petitions to God on behalf of the Zhuang, the Turkmen, and the Azerbaijani rose with the sun in every time zone, in many languages. Bible translators, Jesus film producers, and others suddenly found these new-style missionaries on their doorsteps, advocating the development, production, and dissemination of these media in little-known languages and offering to find the funds to make it happen. Many of the new-style missionaries succeeded in getting visas as language students. After a year of full-time language learning and culture learning, they began quietly to recruit "tentmakers" (the Apostle Paul's trade), or bivocational workers with marketable skills in medicine, teaching, or engineering who could obtain visas. They convened small, low-profile, international conferences assembling interested parties from around the globe. Ten to twelve missionary-sending nations were represented around an interdenominational conference table, focusing on a specific, neglected people group for the first time. This practice was repeated across the world by these catalysts. They produced a kaleidoscope of caring partnerships, each focusing on one needy people group.

At first these multi-function trailblazers were called "nonresident missionaries" (NRMs) because it was wrongly assumed that most would not be able to live inside these hard-to-enter countries. Because their movements and activities were watched too closely inside the country, the NRMs established their base of operations in nearby nations, itinerated in the designated homeland, and traveled elsewhere to the worldwide resources needed for the task. When marketable skills and language-learning visas helped many NRMs establish residence in heretofore uncharted territory, the concept evolved. These workers' titles went from NRMs to SCs (strategy or strategic coordinators), still maintaining their mobility when needed, doing the same job but living inside the homeland—if conditions allowed for relatively free flow of communications.

Keith Parks loved this innovative approach. It spoke to his creative side and to his decades-long passion for cracking the remaining barriers to fulfillment of the Great Commission. One of his favorite books during this period was Scott Peck's *The Road Less Traveled*. For Parks, this bestseller seemed to speak to his own great desire to break out of ineffective patterns. "You're not doing enough," he would tell missionaries, "because you're not failing enough." Prior to this time, most missions leaders everywhere assumed that a truly worldwide sharing of the gospel would have to wait until so-called "closed" countries evolved toward friendlier, more open governments allowing traditional missionary work to commence.

The revolutionary approach Parks championed was designed to work with the worldwide status quo. Instead of waiting on Islamic republics and Communist-controlled states to change their policies toward religion and outsiders, innovative Christian workers could pierce the walls with brand new strategies not requiring immediate entry. Despite misgivings and objections from some FMB administrators in some parts of Asia, he gave the SC program his constant, faithful support with the budget and personnel needed. He was available to advise, to pray for, and to encourage in other ways these new-style missionaries. He exchanged correspondence with them and took up their causes when middle managers in the organization erected roadblocks.

Also during this time Parks named Catherine Walker, retired missionary in China and Indonesia, to lead intercessory prayer efforts at the FMB. She was followed by Minette Drumwright, who had labored faithfully for years as a mission activist in Texas before joining the Board's staff a few years before the prayer office appointment. Her new assignment gave a major boost to the launching of the pioneer missionaries' promotion of unevangelized people groups among Southern Baptists. Suddenly bursting on the SBC scene were reports on ethnic groups such as the Kazakhs and the Kurds, who had been previously unknown to most people in the pews. "PrayerGrams" and a toll-free "Prayer Line" made household words out of the exotic-sounding names of these people groups.

What made all this so revolutionary in the history of Christian missions? Few mission societies or denominations could afford to assign missionaries who didn't seem to be "hands-on" workers in the mission field. In those faith groups missionaries were dependent upon what they could personally raise in direct, face-to-face appeals to a limited number of congregations. What congregation was going to give funds to support such a strange enterprise? In the early days of such a program most would scratch their heads, turn their backs to it, and look for a traditional missionary to support.

Since Southern Baptists pooled their resources for missionary support through annual budgets of local churches, with missions money going to the Cooperative Program, this new brand of Christian ambassador wouldn't have to go around raising a salary to do an untried work. Parks could afford to experiment, to give the new model a chance to prove itself.

Until that time in Christian mission history, most missionary endeavors took the path of least resistance. If a government of a given country prohibited Christian missionaries from working within its borders, the mission would go elsewhere. With Parks' new strategy, borders did not matter. If traditional Christian work was ruled out, a different approach was called for to accomplish the same purpose. Did that nation need engineers? Did it need medical workers? A separate organization would be *created*, not *tied to* a Christian name, through which missionary engineers and missionary medical workers would be deployed. If entry still proved difficult, missionaries would work from outside the border, mobilizing prayer, short-wave radio program producers and non-American foreigners who were able to obtain visas.

Parks constantly reminded all the decision makers, beginning at the FMB (now International Mission Board, IMB), then at CBF and in the churches across the country: "These unevangelized peoples have no advocates; they cannot send a representative to your mission council meeting to plead for part of your resources. Who will speak for them? We must resist the local pressures that would siphon funds away from those of World A."

World A is a term coined to describe the fifth of the world's population having little or no access to the gospel in language and in cultural expression it could best understand. (Others use the term "10-40 Window," the rectangular area in latitudes north of the equator covering North Africa and a fair part of Asia.) The Kurds provide an example of a World A population segment. They have no Kurdish church buildings in their sections of Syria, Iraq, Iran, and Turkey. They have little or no Christian radio in their dialects, only portions of the Scriptures in the various dialects, and few Kurdish believers openly espousing the Christian cause. World B is the near-half of the world having the opportunity to hear but not yet responding (for example, Japan). World C has the gospel and shares it with the other "worlds."

It was those who haven't had an opportunity to hear the gospel (Rom 15:20-21) who occupied Parks' thoughts and activities day and night. Single-mindedness best described him. This was "the overriding quality," CBF missionary "T" Thomas said, "that seems to set Keith apart from so many for me." Sitting in Parks' office one day, Thomas commented on "the numerous barriers that would be involved if CBF committed a missionary to work among those of a certain unevangelized people group." Parks' response: "Forget the difficulties for a moment and ask yourself what you could do if God put all His resources (people, prayer, and funds) at your disposal? How would you proceed then?" "He taught me," Thomas recounted, "that this is how we must plan and proceed, trusting that the Lord will give us all that we need to accomplish the task."

Parks was a news addict. He stayed abreast of world developments by consulting the Internet at home in the evenings, seldom going to bed before 11:30. His world vision gave him the motivation to keep going, persevering longer than much younger men on the road, traveling every weekend and often on weekdays. Staff members shook their heads in weary amazement at this seventy-one-year-old's giving sharp attention to detail during late evening conferences at the Fellowship's offices on the Atlanta campus of Mercer University.

His single-mindedness earlier at the FMB did not have quite the effect on the large organization as it did later at CBF. Other global needs could still be addressed adequately at the Board. The FMB did seem to try to address them all, at least during Parks' administration. It could do so because it was the largest Protestant dispatcher of career missionaries in the world. Its annual Christmas offering alone (approximately $100 million in the late 1990s) outstripped the budget of some small nations' governments.

Parks' single-minded vision impacted the life of an organization most at the Cooperative Baptist Fellowship from 1993 to 1999 with his presence and surely for many years into the future. The positive side of this was obvious. CBF became a significant player on the stage of frontier missions into the twenty-first century. The negative side was partly a function of the Fellowship's short history and of its size.

Since Parks was given the authority and full support of the earliest CBF missions committee and of the Fellowship's first Coordinator, Cecil Sherman, his early decisions and ongoing objectives could be based simply on his own vision and long, effective track record. Granted, his was similar in outline to what the first committee envisioned, but Parks significantly shaped it. The positive result was World A advocacy and action. The negative aspect, some critics would say, was the refusal to engage in a substantive way most of the crying needs elsewhere. True, CBF developed ministries to refugees, immigrants, the homeless, and AIDS victims in certain cities. The number of opportunities he declined to pursue, however, outnumbered those he embraced.

To such criticism Parks responded by noting that CBF was too young and too small to be all things to all people; it could not plant its flag everywhere. Those who saw it differently argued that not every Christian was led by God to engage World A. Who was Keith Parks, they would grumble, that he should keep CBF global mission resources from ministering to street children in South America or refugees in Africa?

Indeed, Parks' power to steer the ship was felt much more strongly in the CBF movement than in his earlier years at the top of the huge Foreign Mission Board. Thus, when parts of Central America were destroyed in late 1998 by Hurricane Mitch, the response from Atlanta's CBF office left much to be desired. Parks put out the word that any contributions members wanted to give toward needs in Nicaragua and among its neighbors could be sent directly to the Baptist World Alliance (or forwarded by CBF to the BWA), which in turn would work through local Baptists in the devastated region. One could only do so much and in so few places, the rationale ran; let the coffers of the IMB or of other agencies provide substantive help to Central America. Parks, though expressing concern and interest (commenting privately on IMB aid plans), preferred leading CBF elsewhere, among those having no advocates at all. The results were dramatic for the recipients in a positive way; for critical observers, it modeled a Christian discipleship out of balance with world-wide realities and less than proactive for most arenas other than World A's.

How was it that this son of a small Texas cattle trader, this man who, in his younger years became ill when given responsibility, sick to his stomach when facing conflict, developed into the pioneer destined to have as great an impact as any Baptist missions leader in the twentieth century? What made it possible for him to withstand unrelenting, steadily increasing, and often unwarranted crit-icism? And what drove a man to cross perilous frontiers, such as the Syrian-Iraqi border, well beyond the normal retirement age?

Chapter 2

From the Texas Plains to Indonesia's Islands

If the Parks' dog hadn't bitten me, I wouldn't be a Christian today!

—Indonesian convert,
nursed to health and faith by Parks

"Son," the father of the young Baptist Student Union (BSU) president said, "I don't know much about college, but I don't think it's supposed to make you sick."

Parks suffered from a bad case of the nervous stomach. He took too seriously his new responsibility as president of the BSU at North Texas State College (now University) in Denton in 1947–1948. At the moment there was no campus minister, and Parks mistakenly assumed too much responsibility for the spiritual life on campus. (He could laugh years later in recounting that after his election he purchased a pair of black shoes he thought appropriate for his new responsibilities.) What also came with the role was a persistent nervous stomach. By the end of the year, he was still far from being at peace.

When he went home that summer to his parents' farm at Corinth near Danville, Arkansas, he sought advice from his dad, who worked hard as a rancher and competed honestly and effectively with dishonest traders at auction. "Daddy wanted to show people," Parks told writer Robert O'Brien, "that an honest man could out-trade the shysters in the business. He was known for his integrity. If a man died and left a widow with cattle, she would call Bob Parks and say, 'I know I can trust you to sell these for me.'" Pride in his work gave Bob a self-confident attitude his son had yet to learn. His comment to Keith, that higher education was not supposed to be hazardous to his health, proved to be the jolt the younger Parks needed.

Working with two mules on the farm that summer, he thought more about it all as he moved across the fields. He concluded he shouldn't take the entire student body's spiritual fate as his personal responsibility. "I really wasn't in charge of things," he realized, and told himself: "Let the Lord take care of things." Later he would take on the entire world with grace and wit as leader of the largest Protestant mission agency. That early burden, however, never quite left him. As he would tell missionaries as late as June 1998: "We have a heavy responsibility. We are to be, in some ways, the personification of Jesus Christ in the situation in which we minister. The business we're about is an awesome activity that the Lord has given us."

For a man of hardy constitution who set foot in more than 100 countries, his earlier years seemed to offer no grounds for predicting the healthy, robust life he would live. Robert Keith Parks was born 23 October 1927 in Memphis, Texas, two years before the stock market crash. He contracted rheumatic fever at age six and suffered pain in his knees and hips for several years. The doctor said he wouldn't live to age thirteen. His parents, Bob and Allie Parks, prayed, "Lord, if you will spare him, we'll do all we can to prepare him to serve you." (Keith did not learn of their prayer until his senior year of high school when he dedicated his life to the ministry.) His family included two older sisters and a younger brother. They had few material possessions, partly because his parents were in debt over Keith's hospital bills and over the economic effects of the Great Depression.

At age ten he moved with the family to Gravelly, Arkansas, one year after his conversion and baptism. His dad, a former football player, worked the cattle auctions in Fort Smith. He could be stern in some ways, but Keith remembered only one spanking. His loving mother never showed anger; everything was always alright, despite the financial difficulties and the successive moves from Memphis (Texas), to Gravelly, and to Corinth, Arkansas. Instead of talking with family members about their differences, she would discuss it with God alone. As a result, Parks received a solid foundation in many ways, but he did not learn at a young age how to manage conflict.

Although his dad had helped him get over his nervous stomach at college, Parks would find the constructive handling of crises and conflict an elusive goal until he had gone through his first term of missionary service in Indonesia and received counseling and insight during a Clinical Pastoral Education course he took while on furlough. (He did have some early success, however, in handling pressure-filled situations by sharing leadership of North Texas State's national-championship debate team.) According to long-time friend Bill O'Brien (no blood relation to Robert O'Brien), in an unpublished essay about Parks,

> It was at North Texas that a community of Baptist believers, and particularly the Baptist Student Union, began to impact Parks at the point of his own giftedness and calling. The woman who was campus minister saw in Keith something he had never seen in himself, and she began to confront him with the claims of God on his life.
>
> One particular experience stands out. In meditation and prayer Keith describes the impression that God was asking him if he would be willing to do whatever God requested. His initial response was, "Tell me what it is." Only after much soul-searching he realized the only answer he could give to God's question was "yes." Only with his willingness to do whatever God was asking would God reveal what it was Keith should do. It was soon evident some form of vocational Christian ministry was the framework of the calling.

During his college years Parks tried his hand as an evangelist. He worked with various students; one preached, and the other led the music. They conducted week-long revival services whenever school schedules allowed. Although he was active in the church, he somehow escaped a call to missions until seminary. This never ceased to amaze him in later life, that he could have gone so long without a connection to the heartbeat of Southern Baptists—missions.

"The Lord called me to missions after I graduated from college," Parks shared in testimony to various audiences. "I didn't have a clue about missions." That astounded him as he reflected on it many years later. Despite all the Baptist life he had already experienced, Parks realized later it had not occurred to him there were people who had never heard the gospel, until a summer mission trip in 1948 to San Andres Island, Colombia. He ministered that summer to descendants of British slaves, returned to Texas with an enlarged view of the world, and enrolled at Southwestern Baptist Theological Seminary, Fort Worth, Texas. There, missions-minded professors' lectures and chapel sermons helped solidify his sense of call to missions.

At a BSU state convention he met Helen Jean Bond of Abilene, Texas. Not until later at Southwestern would it occur to him she might someday be his wife. It took all his persuasive powers because another missions volunteer had been dating the former student minister (who continued commuting to the Rice University campus in Houston to witness and to disciple students). "I convinced her of the error of her ways (dating the other guy)," he recalled with a smile. They sat beside each other in a church administration class at seminary and then started dating in December. The next May they were engaged, and a year later were married on 24 May 1952, two years before their appointment as Southern Baptist missionaries. Keith had committed himself to missions at Southwestern's Missions Day when Professor Jack MacGorman preached. Parks received his Bachelor of Divinity degree and advanced to the Doctor of Theology degree, also from Southwestern, granted after he went overseas.

From his first seminary days Parks had a passion "to scrape away" the unbiblical layers of Christianity. Through the centuries churches had constructed many traditions around the concept of *ecclesia*, the "called-out ones" who formed the first assemblies, congregations, or churches in New Testament days. Parks' love of simplicity caused him to search for the core beliefs. "The bare minimum" for a congregation, he concluded, was:

- acknowledgement of Jesus Christ as Lord—"the only creed I'm comfortable with"
- discovery of some way to get together for worship—"the desire for fellowship somehow built into conversion"
- church discipline to protect themselves from violating the fellowship

Later on the mission field he would put these principles to practice in a successful church-planting program utilizing Indonesian seminary students.

During his own seminary doctoral studies in the United States, Parks taught a New Testament course and Homiletics at Hardin-Simmons University in Abilene, where Helen Jean's father taught English. First Baptist Church in Abilene was Helen Jean's home church. "She became Helen Jean Parks in Abilene, and Keith improved his standing in the community immediately," recalled Bill Bruster, who served ten years as pastor there. "The two of them have long been loved and revered in Abilene, and especially in First Baptist Church."

Parks also served as pastor from 1950 to 1954 of "the best church in the world," Red Springs Baptist Church, a rural congregation 150 miles west of Fort Worth. (His first son Randall, who was born during that time, would later serve the same church during his own graduate student days at Southwestern.) The date for departure for the mission field arrived while Parks labored to wrap up his commitments. He finished editing his doctoral dissertation at 2 AM and left for the mission field at 6 AM. "I wanted it to be a fresh document," he said with a wide grin.

While Keith had heard about the needs in Indonesia from the FMB's Elmer West at a Fort Worth meeting, Helen Jean had stayed in Abilene, pregnant with their first child, Randall. Keith was excited about the prospect of serving in a seminary abroad. At first, Helen Jean was not too thrilled about a place called Indonesia, not realizing that it was the name of the newly independent nation. When she saw a newsreel about Mount Merapi's volcanic eruption, Helen Jean learned that Java ranked, at that time, as the most densely populated place in the world. The Indonesians on the screen looked like her Hawaiian and Filipino friends.

"We were driving home that night," Keith recalled in a Martha Skelton interview for *The Commission* magazine, "and she said, 'I believe the Lord's calling us to Indonesia.' I said, 'Good. He called me last September. I'm glad you're going along!' "

The Indonesia of 1954 had not yet developed into one of the economic "tigers" of Asia. Western fast food, shopping malls, and world-class hotels were still more than a generation away. Yet the young Parks family (one-year-old Randall in tow) was assigned a comfortable house with a garden in the green hills of Bandung, a quiet town of slightly cooler temperatures on the island of Java.

The Parks applied themselves full-time to acquisition of a relatively simple Malay dialect ("Indonesian," the official government language) that first year. The Baptist Mission, the organization of Southern Baptist missionaries who had transferred to Indonesia from China in 1952, then assigned the Parks as originally planned to Semarang, on Java's northern coast, to teach at the seminary for Indonesian pastors in training.

Quickly, Parks was thrust into increased responsibility, preparing lesson plans in a foreign language, teaching classes, helping to manage the seminary, and relating to local churches. He ran a successful evangelism effort by dispatching students to help start churches with few resources. Those good times were accompanied by the tensions of developing a new seminary, growing pains of the new Baptist Mission (organization of Southern Baptist missionaries in the country), and conflict with local Communist labor leaders. Helen Jean was trying to balance responsibilities of a very young, growing family and of an authentic missionary calling of her own. They did not handle all the stress from different directions as constructively as they desired.

On their first furlough in the United States, Keith was asked to work as a missionary consultant with the FMB's Personnel Department and was encouraged to receive training in Clinical Pastoral Education (CPE). During the training they realized that patterns from their own upbringing were being repeated in their individual ways of coping with conflict. Both found that they had not been responding in healthy ways to everyday pressures. (At that time also they were coping with their son Kent's two-year bout with tuberculosis.) The course helped them to relate appropriately to each other and to strengthen their marriage.

"When Helen Jean would say something that really bothered me," Keith remembered, "I would withdraw. She

would ask later if something was troubling me, and I would
deny it. I had been taught growing up that you don't talk
about it, that it was up to the other person to confess and
make amends. Helen Jean came from a family where everyone spoke their mind very openly, nothing personal
intended. We had to learn to separate the emotional aspect
of conversations. It helped us tremendously on the mission
field and in our marriage. Since then we've always recommended CPE to other ministers and missionaries."

Parks learned those lessons well. After his first furlough
he grew increasingly adept in receiving and benefiting from
criticism. He seldom took it personally when opponents,
whether they be Communists in Indonesia or fundamentalists in America, blistered him with their attacks against his
leadership, philosophy, and policies. "I really profited in this
respect by dealing with local Communist labor leaders in
Indonesia." After those experiences he was prepared to deal
with confrontation and battles of the minds among missionaries or denominational leaders. Many years later in
Richmond, Virginia, at the FMB's headquarters on tree-
lined Monument Avenue, a hostile trustee on the board of
directors would ask, "Keith, don't you realize there are a lot
of people out there who don't like you?" Yes, he had recognized that, but he had learned to separate the role from the
person, not to take it personally.

Along with Catherine Walker, Keith Parks pioneered the
use of Clinical Pastoral Education at the Indonesian seminary and served as interim president for the school. He also
continued to spearhead evangelistic "probe efforts" with
seminary students in unchurched areas of north central
Java. The students called this outreach "dropping," because
of the method of leaving student evangelists at strategic
points in a prearranged circuit, with the Holy Spirit, a Bible,
and usually little else.

"The activity proved to be the kind of indigenous vehicle that was used by the Spirit of God," O'Brien once wrote about Parks' program with the seminary students. "In each location where students would work, they could count on an average of about fifty professions of faith, with at least half of them sticking. One group returned from their labors reporting they had started in seven other places. People rode bicycles long distances to hear the witness of the students, and then returned witnessing to their own villages where the gospel had not been heard before."

Meanwhile, Parks was learning to leave his heavy duties at the office in those days as a young parent. When he reached the confines of his missionary residence, Parks was able to focus on his growing family. Helen Jean gave birth to their second child, Kent, in 1957, and to Eloise in 1961. Stan completed the family in 1963, the year before they left Semarang. In addition to devoting himself to work and family, Parks found time to write his first book, *Crosscurrents*, published by Convention Press in 1966. The missions study focused on Bangladesh, India, and other Asian nations where Southern Baptist missionaries were starting new ministry. Although he had been asked to write the book, no budget had been allocated for travel or research. Parks dipped into his personal savings to visit the sites.

In their early years in Indonesia, the Parks found acceptance of the sheer mass of humanity to be one of the biggest adjustments. There seemed to be no respite from the press of crowds, the lack of privacy on the densely populated island of Java. For a break they would go to the harbor of Semarang, rent a sailboat with a two-man crew, and enjoy their picnic offshore as a family. "This is the only way we can be alone as a family," Keith remarked to Helen Jean during one of the outings. She looked around them, noting the two Indonesian boatsmen, and said, "Yeah, right."

Parks himself displayed a sense of humor that was becoming famous. His witty one-liners and quick retorts won him friends far and wide. Referring to his baldness, he said, "The heads God was ashamed of, He covered up." Humor gave him "a sense of balance," Helen Jean said. "As long as I've been married to him, I still am not always sure when he is joking and kidding about something because he can do it with such a straight face."

Parks enjoyed playing practical jokes, too. He would let visiting missionary guests think there was someone outside the Parks' guestroom window at night, when it was really the family's talking mynah bird! Besides exotic birds there are also, of course, exotic fruits in Southeast Asia. One peculiar fruit is called "durian." Good-tasting but foul-smelling, durian is banned on airplanes and in other public confines. One evening at a conference Parks and other missionaries arranged to have some of the fruit placed under the bed of a visitor from the U.S. It took some time for the smell to dissipate and for the guest to forgive what had happened.

Confession and forgiveness were features of the Indonesian Revival of the 1960s, which filled thousands of island churches with new believers. Political, economic, and social forces, especially the violent reaction against Communism, worked hand in hand with the Holy Spirit to cause remarkable conversions. It also affected the Baptist Mission in that sprawling nation. At its annual meetings and at other gatherings, missionaries confessed their sins to one another, sought reconciliation, and experienced personal and corporate revival.

Parks discovered renewal at these times, but he also found it in a different, more individualized way. Back in his first term of service in Indonesia, when he was interim president of the seminary, he learned a lesson about waiting and resting on the Lord's strength. One afternoon he lay on a shaded bamboo bench on the Semarang campus, resting momentarily from the tropical heat. He had been frustrated and irritated, barely controlling his anger as he dealt with a persistent relational problem with some students and seminary employees. Suddenly, the well-known Bible verse (Isa 40:31) about waiting on the Lord came to mind. Parks later described it as being almost an audible voice, followed by a personalized word to him in his situation: "Show the love of Jesus, or go home." It struck deep within him. Unless he could show the unconditional love of Christ in his relationships with difficult students, pastors, missionaries, and Communist labor leaders, he had no business on the mission field. It proved to be another life-changing moment for him.

Other lives were changing, too, sometimes in unexpected ways. One Indonesian man testified at the local Baptist church: "If Parks' dog hadn't bitten me, I wouldn't be a Christian today." The man had heard that westerners were cruel and harsh, but Parks changed that perception when he personally doctored the man's wounds and took him to a physician. Afterwards, Parks invited him to church, where he eventually became a Christian.

A Muslim minister of religious affairs on the island of Java found himself one morning on a day-long train trip in a crowded railcar, knee to knee with a foreigner named Keith Parks. The high official, apparently not an Islamic fundamentalist, soon made it clear that he believed there was no essential difference between Christianity and Islam. He did not know, however, if God had forgiven his sin; one had to hope that his good deeds would outweigh his bad. Parks, in turn, sought common ground in the story of Adam and Eve and the tree of the knowledge of good and evil.

"We both have a tree of sin growing out of our hearts," Parks said, proceeding to share testimony of how God had

uprooted the tree of sin and planted a tree of life in his own
heart. Tears welled up in the eyes of the Javanese official.
After a silent moment, he said, "I wish I could believe that."

A relationship that flourished was the Parks' friendship
with an Indonesian university vice president, a Javanese
Christian who tutored Keith and Helen Jean in the language.
In the early days of their friendship the Parks astounded
their new friends by inviting their whole family to join the
Parks family on a picnic. It was the first time these Indonesians had gone together as a family on such an outing.
Lack of transport had made it difficult for a family with
eight children. The Parks' gesture of hospitality cemented
what became a rich, long friendship. The insights gained
from this family through long talks helped Keith and Helen
Jean to understand more fully the worldview of Indonesians
and to interpret the Christian faith to Asians in a more
culturally appropriate way.

What did not seem to fit the culture, in Parks' view, were
institutions under foreign control. Parks saw the way they
stifled creativity, drained resources, and decreased missionary mobility. Tied to the maintenance of schools and other
buildings and staffs, missionaries realized their budgets and
their ministries were wrapped up almost completely in the
life of the institutions. As a result, they had few resources left
with which to respond to new opportunities. Strategic decisions were based too frequently on real estate concerns
rather than on spiritual priorities. For the next three decades
Parks would resist the proliferation of brick and mortar as a
strategy and invest more in personal ministries. His long-
held desire to simplify "church" fueled the student
evangelism and new mission initiatives he fostered. By
churches he meant born-again believers, not buildings,
Spirit-led assemblies and not property-conscious pew-
sitters. The seeds were planted for what would become

Parks' rallying cry as an international missions leader: "Evangelism resulting in churches."

"We will never do less than this," he often said. "We will always do more than this." Medical work, community development, and many other ministries played important roles. In addition to their own merits in addressing human needs as a whole, these skills opened doors in countries closed to preachers.

Missionary Keith Parks and a seminary student visit the home of a Christian family in Indonesia in 1957. (Photo courtesy, Fon H. Scofield, Jr., SBC Foreign Mission Board)

Missionary Keith Parks witnesses to laborers in Indonesia in 1957. (Photo courtesy, Fon H. Scofield, Jr., SBC Foreign Mission Board)

Chapter 3

Missionary on Administrative Assignment

The key to finding God's will is the commitment to do it before we know what it is.

—Keith Parks

"I never saw myself as giving up my missionary calling when elected to take up administrative roles," Parks said, when asked whether he missed the missionary ministries he enjoyed for fourteen years. "I've always considered myself to be a missionary. It just happens that I'm now a missionary on administrative assignment."

Crossing that boundary, however, from field missionary to home office representative called for discernment of God's will. Often he was asked by Baptists across the U.S. and overseas, "How do I know God's will?"

"The key to finding God's will," he would frequently respond to candidates for missionary service, "is the commitment to do it before we know what it is." He added, "It's not a one-time thing, and thus God's will also calls for a commitment to follow, knowing it changes in the course of a Christian's pilgrimage."

He cautioned missionary candidates to avoid the tendency to think they alone could discern God's will. "The spiritual response of that will has to be done in the context of community," he noted, citing the example of the church in Antioch that sought God's will regarding the setting apart of its first missionaries (Acts 13). "The balance of individual going and collective sending is a beautiful and spiritual balance," Parks said.

Dealing with young Southern Baptists interested in serving as missionaries was not always a heavy, serious enterprise. During one furlough from Indonesia, Parks served in the FMB's Missionary Personnel Department. Part of his responsibility was to help interview candidates for missionary service. He remembered one woman who seemed to deny any anger over her husband's domineering ways. Parks kept probing to determine if, indeed, she was in denial about how her husband really affected her. (The Board, of course, wanted its missionaries to have strong, healthy marriages that could withstand new pressures in crosscultural situations.)

With every response the lady denied any resentment toward her husband's tendencies to try to control her life. "Don't you ever want to do something to 'get back' at your husband?" Parks finally asked. After a hesitant moment of silence, the would-be missionary replied, "Well, sometimes, after he leaves to go to work, I take his toothbrush and swish it in the toilet bowl!" Although he enjoyed the work, after a year in the Personnel Department, Parks was eager to return to ministry overseas.

In his third term of service in Indonesia, this time in the capital of Jakarta as government liaison and mission treasurer, roles Parks never had imagined filling, he witnessed the bloody riots following the attempted coup d'état on 30 September 1965. Most westerners shut down operations, left the island, or shut themselves indoors. Calmer heads knew from experience that such incidents were usually localized; taking timely detours made daily business a bit slower but still sustainable. "There was only one day I didn't go to the Mission office," Parks recalled. "You could find circuitous routes to take."

Those terrible days, however, were not like the usual Third World outbursts to which missionaries and others have grown accustomed. In Indonesia, there occurred some of the bloodiest days in history, with an estimated 200,000 to 500,000 Communists and others killed on some of the most populated of the nation's islands. The phone system was destroyed, and the currency system was in shambles. With no established rate for currency, Parks and others had to resort temporarily to seeking out daily the Chinese traders around the city to negotiate rates.

In 1968 Keith Parks was elected by FMB trustees to become area secretary (later called "area director") for Southeast Asia after Winston Crawley vacated the post to become director of the Board's Overseas Division. This meant returning to Richmond, Virginia, to the headquarters on Monument Avenue. For the next seven years Parks supervised Southern Baptist mission work in Thailand, Malaysia, Indonesia, the Philippines, and Vietnam in an ever-expanding arc across the region. He served as the strategic liaison between the Board and the missionaries. Those most recent years as treasurer for the Indonesian Mission had helped prepare him for the task of examining proposed mission budgets and of interpreting policy. The earlier years in the field, teaching and helping churches grow, gave Parks the background necessary to lead hundreds of missionaries in Asia to formulate effective strategies, including the tasks of identifying field needs and prioritizing their lists of personnel requests for new missionary candidates to consider. His was a pivotal role for a major bloc of nations. His time in airplanes began to increase.

"Though he traveled 30 to 50 percent of the time when the kids were growing up," Helen Jean recalled, "when he was home, he was there '150 percent'," attending the children's programs, recitals, and sporting events.

On the road Parks tried his best to lead missionaries to find consensus on issues. Whenever possible he would force the decision making back on the local missions. One good missionary friend grew frustrated with Parks' approach. "Just tell us what to do!" she pleaded. Parks laughed. He explained that she would gladly have him do so on the issue at hand, but when they would disagree on future issues, she and others would be angry with him if he made the decision instead of leaving it to the missionaries.

Within two years of his election as area secretary, Parks saw his dream of decentralized training become a reality. He had pushed for more Theological Education by Extension (T.E.E.) on mission fields in lieu of centralized Bible schools and seminaries. In this type of training, without leaving their communities, more young ministers could receive simplified, programmed instruction materials and weekly, small-group, student sessions led by a missionary or senior pastor. (Often those who had gone to the big city for training in a comfortable residential program had refused to return to the less exciting life in a village or small town.) The Baptist missionaries in Indonesia, emboldened by spiritual renewal that greatly affected Parks, too, voted to shut down the seminary for a while and devote more energies to T.E.E., personal evangelism, and discipleship. They also pledged to rededicate themselves to simpler lifestyles, identifying more with the people and less with other expatriates, possibly selling some of the larger houses of the old colonial era.

The bold move, strongly endorsed by Parks, proved controversial in Indonesia and throughout the region, not to mention back at FMB headquarters in Richmond, Virginia. Many missionaries felt they had sacrificed enough just by leaving extended families in America. Suggesting to them that they should also live simpler lifestyles was always sure to cause anger and a rebellious attitude among some of them. Also, traditions died hard. Making a sudden change as significant as closing the seminary raised questions among national believers and among home office administrators, including Executive Secretary Baker James Cauthen. Poor communications in those days prior to easy e-mail did not help in Parks' efforts to win home-office affirmation. Extension centers finally won the day, demonstrating their effectiveness, but the seminary was also restored.

The concept of extension centers spread to other Asian nations where former missionaries to China had transferred. In Vietnam, there was much pressure to deemphasize church planting and concentrate more on alleviation of suffering in this war-ravaged country. Parks continued, however, to push church development as the best way to help the Vietnamese. Ministry to physical needs such as providing medicine, shelter, meals, and clothes would be developed primarily with the local churches' resources and low-profile missionary aid. This stance represented Parks' preference throughout his career, a philosophy favored by more conservative Baptists but disliked by those wanting a higher priority for social ministry, for an expression of God's love without having to tie it to preaching.

One April day when the Parks family was visiting Manila, they witnessed flagellation of Filipinos as part of the Easter demonstration in the city. Helen Jean and the four children stayed back, but Keith wanted to see it up close. The pressure of the crowd almost caused him to fall, though he, at six feet in height, was taller than most Filipinos. Penitent pilgrims marched past the crowds, their backs shredded by lashes from whips. Parks was splattered with blood. Vendors in the street continued their trading.

"This is what it must have been like at the crucifixion," he thought. "People went about their business, buying and selling, amidst the tragedy." His missionary resolve grew stronger. It would be needed for bigger tests in the months and years ahead.

After seven years of leading all Southern Baptist mission work in Southeast Asia, in 1975 Parks was named to direct the Mission Support Division of the FMB. He followed the highly popular Jesse Fletcher who would later become president of Hardin-Simmons University. The administrative unit for which Parks was now responsible housed the departments for personnel, denominational relations, and communications, including missions education and promotion.

"One could assume," wrote Bill O'Brien in his unpublished August 1992 paper about Parks, "the fire burning for the unreached around the world might dim with this assignment. But not so. It was an opportunity to keep Southern Baptists focused on the highest priority of the Kingdom: the mission of God." By the spring of 1976, Parks had reorganized the division and demonstrated a knack for attracting top talent.

His department directors, who would later play pivotal roles in his presidency, included Bill O'Brien and Bill Marshall. They and others were chosen in part because of their ability to work well on a team. "Team" would play an increasingly essential role in Parks' thinking, first at the FMB and later at the CBF. The concept of a cooperative culture would become the central feature of his administrative philosophy. (At CBF it became a high-risk effort to avoid hierarchical layers of field administration. Self-managed field teams were to attempt to provide sufficient accountability for their members, without a field supervisor or regional director. They answered directly to the small Atlanta staff.)

What FMB trustees saw in the earliest efforts impressed them. "It was," wrote Bill O'Brien in an unpublished essay, "as if the last piece of background and experience had been placed in the big picture to bring Parks to the role of the chief steward of the foreign mission endeavor." As the time for Baker James Cauthen's retirement drew near, Parks' name seemed to appear on everyone's shortlist of nominees to succeed the highly respected executive director. (Parks would later lead the trustees to approve a corporate model, with the title of president.) Jesse Fletcher, often in the past considered a prime candidate to succeed Cauthen, declined consideration.

In those awkward days of transition, with speculation mounting into the hot summer of 1979, Parks was told one day that the search committee was summoning him. "Let them get their own coffee!" he replied with a humble laugh. It turned out that the committee wanted far more than refreshment for its members. It wanted fresh winds to blow through the Board's Richmond offices and around the world. Cauthen's illness in his last years in office resulted in some bottlenecks in the decision making essential for Bold Mission Thrust to advance. Since Parks had been loyal to Cauthen, would he be just another "company man" who maintained the status quo?

He was ultimately chosen with trustees' unanimity after many months of deliberation, and he took the reins on the first day of 1980, little more than two months after his fifty-second birthday. His task was to follow in the footsteps of Baker James Cauthen. Parks had been in awe of Cauthen, whom he considered "a charismatic leader in the most wholesome sense of that word." Like Cauthen, Parks would become a beloved preacher who, as he had described Cauthen, also "just lived and breathed missions, and everywhere he went he created a great enthusiasm." Christian missions would see a new day during the next twelve years, especially during the second half of Parks' tenure.

After his election one staff member said, "Keith, I didn't think you were the right one for the job, but I want you to

know that I'll now support you in every way." Some leaders
would have promptly written off the forthright employee.
Parks' response was to name him later to a key role in his
administrative team, a function the staffer retained after
Parks' departure in 1992.

That move epitomized the approach of the Board's new
leader. He did not feel threatened by the talent around him;
he welcomed it and encouraged all to speak their minds.
Parks had a simple, matter-of-fact way with people, trusting
them to do their jobs. "The joy of serving under the leadership of Keith Parks," notes CBF missionary Lonnie Turner,
"is to experience the empowerment and trust he gives to do
ministry in an atmosphere of freedom, creativity, vision, and
even disagreement." The Turners, who were FMB missionaries for twenty years in Zambia before joining CBF's team
ministering to the diplomatic community, observed that
they "have served under Keith Parks for twenty-five years—
half of our lives. We believe Keith would say, 'Keep on
serving.'"

Parks was never a "control freak" on routine and daily
ministry, although he could stand very firm on principles
that shaped his philosophy of missions. Rather than micro-
manage his staff, as Cauthen did, he stuck to the big-picture
issues. "I tend to leave staff pretty much on their own," he
wrote to a new addition to his team. "Let us know if you
need any help. We're glad you're here!" This proved to be a
significant shift from Cauthen's era. Although Cauthen was
revered and loved by most missionaries, the gifted leader's
desire to be consulted before almost any action was taken
was well known on the field because of the delays it caused
in the decision-making process. At the same time, one FMB
insider believed, Parks' preference for consensus among his
top administrators "was his greatest weakness." "He was one
of the most effective presidents in FMB history," the staff

member commented, "but he wouldn't make a unilateral decision on matters discussed with the vice presidents." As a result, some critical issues would be postponed or unresolved.

To this day at the FMB, a number of years after his departure, if an election for Board president were held among staff, Parks would win easily. This was the sober assessment of one administrator under both Parks and his FMB successor. He was especially popular among support staff, if not with all top managers. He gently urged staff to drop the "Dr. Parks" and call him "Keith" and constantly deferred to others, virtually never interrupting in group discussions and often speaking last. Anger was seldom seen, and even then might have been more irritation than anything else. He never raised his voice except from a pulpit. The rare moments when he showed emotion were usually in the middle of a formal challenge or charge to new missionaries. Sometimes tears would trickle down his face as he encouraged young couples and single persons to take up the servant's towel as Jesus did (John 13).

According to behavior profiles gleaned from personality tests of staff, Parks' pattern fit that of a creative individual. His personal chart was in the medium range for dominance and influence and higher on steadiness and caution. The mantle of leadership, however, pushed him out of his natural, introverted ways and compelled him to engage actively in the world of missions. This was reflected in his open attitude toward change and his desire to shape the organization into a dynamic and forward-looking force across the earth.

Parks first sought to lead Southeast Asian missions, country by country, toward the cutting edge of missions. When he moved back to the U.S., he reorganized the Missions Support Division, and then as president at the FMB he steered trustees to approve two major reorganizations. The

first reorganizaton moved the FMB to a corporate model
and sought to shore up its financial base with an office of
development. (Throughout his top administrative assignments at the FMB and at CBF, he fought a losing battle over
dwindling percentages of budget for missions.) He named
longtime friend Bill O'Brien, a talented, creative missionary
in earlier years in Indonesia and an administrator with
Parks, to serve as executive vice president. O'Brien was a
visionary, and Parks gave him freedom to exercise his creative impulses. This trait of the FMB president, his openness
to the great gifts God had bestowed upon others, was a sign
of real leadership.

In his personal style for the decision-making process,
Parks went "to the covenant community and to all kinds of
sources," Bill O'Brien said. "He then goes to the mountain or
wherever and prays and cogitates. His is not an individualis-
tic, pietistic method. His is a pattern consistent through the
years." When Parks had received all the data, he usually
stood ready to take his position and show the tenacity necessary to stick with that decision, come what may. At the same
time, O'Brien allowed, "He'd be the first to admit that we
need all the gifts (spiritual and natural, from staff and
beyond) around the table." He constantly asked staff a lot of
questions. "He surrounded himself with people like this, and
was never intimidated." O'Brien gave as an example Johnnie
Johnson Scofield, who served as vice president of communications. O'Brien said Scofield provided the highest
productivity he has ever seen ("and was the best read person
at the Board"). She constantly put new ideas and new reading materials into the hands of the other decision makers at
the Board.

Another key staff person destined to play a major role
with Parks both at the Board and with CBF was Harlan
Spurgeon, a former missionary to Taiwan and Baptist

college president. In January 1983 Parks asked Spurgeon to meet him in St. Louis, where the FMB president offered the tall man from Missouri the post of vice president for human resources. Spurgeon recalled,

> My first impressions had to do with what a fine human being he was. He was kind, open, intelligent, and very observant of all that was going on around him. We settled in that morning at the Day's Inn across from the airport and immediately got down to broad-ranging discussions.
>
> He told me that the fundamentalist-conservatives had begun placing trustees on the board of the FMB, and he needed someone whom he could trust to head up the area of personnel. The new trustees had already become very aggressive in questioning the beliefs of missionary candidates. Dr. Parks had looked up my 1957 statement of beliefs from our missionary file, and wanted to know why I had said that I was "very conservative, but not a fundamentalist." I explained that I grew up in the midst of fundamentalists in southwest Missouri, and I knew the difference.

The conversation between Parks and Spurgeon lasted all day and all evening. They discussed missiology, theology, and the Southern Baptist Convention. Spurgeon soon moved to Richmond.

A strong leader himself in the large Taiwan Baptist Mission, among Missouri Baptists, and at the FMB headquarters in Virginia, Spurgeon called Parks "the finest leader" with whom he has ever worked. He further commented,

> He verbalizes the direction of the organization with clarity. He invites participation of everyone in the conceptualization as well as in the implementation of the dream. He is the most patient leader I have ever seen in listening to all ideas. But when all the information has

been gathered, he has no problem in moving the organization to set out on its course. The one thing that Keith would never tolerate is for someone to question his integrity, and rightly so, for he was always willing to pay the highest price in terms of personal commitment in the cause of missions.

On his first trip to Russia (in 1984), Parks was reading Scott Peck's bestseller, *The Road Less Traveled*, in which Peck posits the thesis that humans aren't open to change because of fear. Parks internalized the message and thought about Bold Mission Thrust. If Southern Baptists were on the right track, how would they know? If they met all their goals, would they have truly shared the gospel with all the world? He came to the realization that drastic changes would be needed, or as Bill O'Brien put it, "The system had to be turned on its head." The old pebble in the pond approach, the ripple effect of starting new work and then moving from border to contiguous border, wouldn't get the job done. How could the chasm be bridged when so much of the world's Christian resources were being hoarded in countries already possessing the gospel? Throughout the trip to Eastern Europe and upon his return to Richmond, Parks processed the book's ideas and picked the brains of his entourage. It was indeed far more than a normal voyage. As Tom Prevost, who served under Parks at both the Board and CBF, said,

> It was kind of a pilgrimage for him. Bold Mission Thrust had been laid on the whole organization in 1976, but Keith was among the first to ask, "What does it really mean to take the gospel to everyone in the world?" It was going to take some kind of quantum leap.

Parks' second reorganization created the Global Strategy Group (GSG), a panel of vice presidents representing each continent's work and other leaders, all of whom were to devote much of their labors to innovative thinking on world evangelization. They were to bring to the table their knowledge, to meet the needs of the gaps worldwide, to channel resources toward the ultimate objective. Cooperative Services International (CSI), the administrative department charged with new strategic models and actions in World A, was represented there by the new vice president Lewis Myers.

"It wasn't easy for Keith administratively," recalled Prevost. "It was going to affect careers and self-understanding of a lot of folks." It proved to be, however, as O'Brien noted, a case where Parks had thought through the issues and was firm in his conviction that the bold administrative moves were worth the costs.

Although this latest set of changes proved that Parks had a high comfort level with paradigm shifts, it caused "change fatigue" on the mission field, where personnel wearied of the Richmond shuffleboard. The result was slow acceptance on the field of some home office ideas such as the controversial 70/30 Plan, which called for Southern Baptist missions abroad to devote 70 percent of their personnel to give at least half their time to field evangelism and church planting. The remaining 30 percent would be set apart for specialists who would continue to devote half or more of their time to medicine, education, media, administration, and other assignments. A number of missionaries rebelled at the idea, thinking it represented a poor understanding of their ministries' value and of the way they shared their faith. The administration in Richmond conceded later that the plan had been poorly communicated.

"That whole 70/30 fiasco ran off the tracks so fast," Bill O'Brien recalled. Instead of the affirmation intended, the action caused the opposite effect. It was interpreted very

unevenly by administrators, depending on their own desires
for their region. Some twisted arms with the new policy; the
reaction was a strong backlash of negative missionary correspondence, some of which spilled into Baptist media in the
U.S. What the GSG really was seeking was a way to assure
that the missions on each overseas field would not allow the
number of specialists to grow to the point that evangelism
and new churches were neglected. Among new missionary
candidates in the U.S., the specialists (medicine, engineering, publications, and so on) responded more quickly to
specific field requests, and thus the lack of new evangelists
and church planters committing to career service could
leave a number of overseas missions populated predominantly by specialists. In addition, in some areas of the world
specialists were encouraged to go into full-time church
planting (especially in highly responsive areas) and to continue seminary training on furlough. This last requirement
came because most specialists did not have a seminary
degree.

Despite the changes, Parks adhered to the plan of the
Southern Baptist Convention's Bold Mission Thrust,
adopted in 1976. He highlighted several principles again and
again throughout the long-term campaign, which was
designed to take the gospel to all the world by the year 2000.
He called for "evangelism that results in churches" to remain
the FMB's primary purpose. He espoused the incarnational
approach, asking trustees never to abandon the commitment to the career or long-term missionary as the pivotal
category of personnel.

Career missionaries were to plant themselves in a foreign
culture, living out the gospel over time with effective acquisition and use of local languages, sharing in ways sensitive to
and appropriate to local cultures. This led to the indigenous
principle, in which new congregations were shaped in ways

natural to their milieu. Musical instruments and rhythms natural to the local people were employed. They were encouraged to write their own hymns or choruses in non-Western styles and to celebrate their newfound joy in God as the Spirit would lead. Missionaries stayed in the background as mentors or coaches, declining pastorates on the field and encouraging young leadership from within the congregations. The mission did not subsidize pastors' salaries in the indigenous approach; local congregations worked at developing their own stewardship in this regard and finding their own means for establishing locales for worship. New fellowships of believers became self-governing, self-supporting, and self-propagating.

Parks' vision for reaching neglected peoples provided the rationale for most objectives and goals of his administrative years. It had a large part to play in his unprecedented elevation of intercessory prayer's profile at the Board. For the first time, a Board office and staff were set apart for this purpose. First it was Catherine Walker, a former missionary to China and Indonesia. After her retirement Minette Drumwright took charge of this major responsibility, harnessing the prayer power of millions of Southern Baptists.

Another accomplishment of those Parks years at the Board was the new Missionary Learning Center, built on farmland donated by Harwood and Louise Cochrane. "He said he would give us a piece of his farm if we would use it for a missionary learning center. It measured about 230 acres (at Rockville, Virginia)." With the leadership of Sam James, a program was conceived according to the Board's needs, and the building was designed to meet requirements for an ideal missionary orientation process. "We wanted to prepare them to understand how you disengage from this culture," Parks explained to Bill Pitts in an oral history taped at Baylor University, Waco, Texas, in October 1997. "It was an effort to prepare (the missionaries) to make the transition to another culture, to create an attitude where they would be able to more quickly and more effectively learn the language." The program also included missiological studies and practical survival tips for different settings around the world.

Another new move, one of the most important decisions Parks ever made, was signing a consultant's contract for Dr. David Barrett, a brilliant Anglican missionary researcher and author. This move was accomplished in 1983 without unanimous support among administrators. Bill O'Brien recalled that Parks and he purposely "created counter-tension within the system" and knew there would be accusations that Parks gave more to this new research project within the Board than to others. Parks did so deliberately, despite the protests, because he believed it was the best move to make to expedite global evangelization; he was willing to "take the heat" from any critics.

By 1986 Parks had agreed to one of Barrett's heartfelt visions, the concept of the nonresidential missionary (NRM). Barrett believed that the so-called closed countries such as Saudi Arabia or Iran could still receive the gospel, even if missionary entry were prohibited. Parks championed the idea, believing that the Great Commission called for the gospel to go to all peoples whether their governments wanted it or not. It was consistent with his own creative impulse and with his willingness to think differently and utilize new approaches.

Few people recognized it then, and few were aware of it more than a decade later, but this administrative move of freeing up personnel and budget to experiment with the new World A strategy unleashed forces that would revolutionize frontier missions well into the twenty-first century. As the twentieth century drew to a close, the number of missionaries serving in the least-evangelized countries—the ones requiring "creative access"—had multiplied many times. They could in large part thank Parks, Barrett, and NRMs (later to be called "SCs," or "strategy coordinators") of the FMB (now IMB), CBF, and of a few other missionary organizations. By the turn of the century, indigenous facilitators or SCs in Asia and in North Africa were riding a second major wave of believers committed to surmount cultural barriers to some of the remaining unevangelized peoples.

What made this simple administrative decision so important? Missionaries no longer had to wait for a government to change its mind about entry of foreign church workers. They could begin immediately to work at overcoming barriers from the outside. They used methods such as the following:

• worldwide intercessory prayer partners
• globetrotting advocacy for a greater share of every missions dollar
• shortwave radio programs
• dubbing of the *Jesus* film in hundreds of languages
• production of audio and video cassettes
• recruitment of Christians with marketable skills to trade for visas
• quiet encouragement of Christians already in place in the homeland of people groups

Excited, eager candidates scrambled to apply for World A mission service, and some missionary veterans already overseas sought transfers to this exciting new work. While some traditionalists were skeptical of it, entrepreneurial ministers jumped in wholeheartedly.

- Lewis Myers, missionary veteran from Vietnam, served as vice president for CSI.

- David Garrison, a young University of Chicago graduate from Arkansas and a former journeyman to Hong Kong, had worked with Barrett on the global database research. He was named to direct the NRM program in its infancy and became an SC, focusing on a North African people group.

- Bill and Susan Smith in Thailand served as the NRM prototypes and would later train scores of new missionaries and transferees.

- When the program proved itself and became part of the normal administrative system in 1992, Mike Stroope, who started CSI's Kurdish ministry, was named director for CSI and, thus, for all World A ministry of the Board in the most restricted-access countries and most neglected people groups.

- Bill Smith and Gary Baldridge, both former NRMs, became Stroope's field associates. Smith supervised strategy coordinators focusing on unreached people groups of East and Southeast Asia, while Baldridge did the same for those addressing needs from the Turkic peoples at the Kazakh-Chinese border to Berber groups in northwest Africa.

    CSI was Cooperative Services International, originally formed to provide English teachers for China. By the time Parks left the FMB, hundreds of missionaries were already deployed in World A through CSI in places where Western workers had rarely, if ever, been seen: Soviet Central Asia, western China, Saudi Arabia, and Afghanistan. Under Stroope's leadership five additional years, the Board's CSI administrative unit would mushroom in an unprecedented explosion of manpower and financial investment.

Other evangelical groups marveled at the change. They found for the first time that Southern Baptists were cooperating and partnering with them, rather than building denominational empires overseas. The strategy coordinators were trained to work with all Great Commission Christians, of any denomination and of any nationality. They sought to assure that by all good means a people group would hear the gospel.

At the same time the new approach to missions was developing, Parks reached out to other Baptists in 1985 and to other missionary-sending agencies of all denominations in 1987. The first consultation featured Baptist leaders from twenty-one countries learning from each other and encouraging one another. FMB Executive Vice President Bill O'Brien "was the moving force on reaching out to other Great Commission Christians" in the next conference two years later, said Harlan Spurgeon, who served as FMB vice president with Parks and later as his chief associate with CBF the first few years before 1996 retirement.

From his earliest experiences in Indonesia, O'Brien developed an appreciation for the good work done by "a lot of good people" other than Baptists. He nurtured these contacts through the years and established a personal, informal, interdenominational network that served Parks well in this latest initiative. Parks and O'Brien brought together executives from twenty U.S. organizations in a forum that provided historic opportunity for creative synergy for the ideas of America's missionary leaders. Friendships begun that day at the Hyatt Hotel near the Dallas-Fort Worth Airport laid the foundation for unprecedented partnership for the remainder of the century and beyond. International mission societies and parachurch groups such as Bill Bright's Campus Crusade for Christ joined forces to integrate campaigns involving prayer, media, and church-planting pursuits. Parks and J. Philip Hogan, head of the Assemblies of God Division of Foreign Missions, found an immediate kinship and later counted each other as good friends. In truth these groups all had much in common, reinforcing each other's basic theologies (for better or for worse).

In 1989 there was an ad hoc consultation in Singapore among Great Commission Christians. One-hundred and fifty organizations having plans for world evangelization were invited. Parks "brought a powerful presentation at that meeting," Bill O'Brien recalled. Afterward, leaders of Wycliffe Bible Translators and the International Bible Society's New International Version talked of how they could work together with the FMB and others. "This is tremendous," the Wycliffe representative said, "We can let you know which languages are coming into production." The International Bible Society said it could print the new translation for Baptist missionaries and others to distribute.

Parks' dream of a missionary enterprise engaging the whole world had come true. For the first time in history no place on earth was capable of remaining completely free of Christian influence. Everyone would have ample opportunity to hear the Good News of Jesus. Parks' constant refrain was a reminder to 14,000,000 Southern Baptists to "keep the whole world in view." This plea he repeated in monthly columns in *The Commission* magazine and in numerous other articles, which were published in book form by New Hope Press in 1987 under the title, *World in View*. It was part of a strategic line of mission books in the AD 2000 Series showcasing the research of David Barrett and others.

What made Parks' role critical was the opposition to the plan among traditionalists, those wanting to stay with the classical approach to missions. Some key veteran missionaries and mission executives opposed the plan from its inception and for more than a decade beyond. They sincerely believed it would fail. They resented its interference in their territories overseas, though a lack of results with traditional methods begged for innovation. Because the new program necessitated the creation of new "platforms" (visa-generating organizations having no obvious religious connotation) to establish residency where missionaries were prohibited, some traditional administrators balked. Such an approach made it very difficult for them to assimilate the new work into their old structures, since normal patterns of communication would endanger the new organisms and reveal their missionary nature to hostile governments. The result was resentment and lack of support for the new work.

It was true that the NRM/SC approach presented a potential threat to the incarnational principle if these missionaries failed to invest themselves in the language and culture of the local people. There would be in the years ahead a constant temptation to neglect this all-important aspect; networking worldwide in an effort to secure resources for "on-the-ground" workers, the strategy coordinators could easily lose touch with the main purpose of sharing the gospel in the mother tongue of the people and in culturally sensitive ways. If that happened, the SCs would lose credibility and then be far less effective, having not much more than a superficial understanding of the very people they were to serve.

For the most part the traditional area directors were good leaders who had given their lives to missions. They knew their work well and carried heavy responsibilities affecting the daily lives and careers of hundreds of

missionary families across half a continent or more. Having
worked openly in areas not hostile to missionary residence,
they did not see the need for the kind of secrecy CSI workers
were employing in efforts to retain visas in nations where
missionaries were prohibited.

The new-style missionaries keenly felt this opposition.
Coupled with the spiritual forces normally marshaled
against missionary endeavors, the in-house protests presented a terrible challenge. It appeared from time to time
that area directors leading traditional missionary work
would eventually win the day, forcing CSI to disband and to
give up its budget and personnel to the usual types of
ministry.

With the strong, unchanging support of Parks, this
amazing work continued to multiply. Without his backing it
would have been quickly dismantled. Thanks to his fidelity
to the concept, the potential for hearing the gospel was realized for hundreds of millions in Asia and North Africa.
These teeming populations, especially the large minorities
having their own language and culture, experienced for the
first time the availability of the gospel in books, videotapes,
and audiotapes from foreign teachers on local contract or
from engineers of multinational corporations and from
emboldened and encouraged Christians of their country. No
longer was the Christian message confined to colonial
tongues or official government languages. Indeed it was a
new day, an historic breakthrough in the long history of
Christian missions.

So strong was the breakthrough in some areas, such as
among Cambodians planting Baptist churches by the dozens
and among Kabyle Berbers transforming their Algerian
mountain communities, that the very people being reached
were soon seen as the ones who would be the most effective
missionaries across still more cultural barriers. World

evangelization no longer seemed to be wishful thinking. In addition to the unprecedented penetration of new frontiers by many Great Commission groups, on the average during Parks' administration Southern Baptists were entering new territories every sixteen weeks, a total of more than fifty countries (more than ten of these were unpublished destinations because of work in sensitive situations with people groups whose governments prohibited missionary work).

As often happens in spiritual matters, the victories gained soon appeared to draw even more opposition. This time the threat came from fellow Baptists, the fundamentalists. Although they espoused missions, they wanted their own leaders to purge Baptist institutions, including the Southern Baptist Foreign Mission Board. The toughest battles of Keith Parks' life lay straight ahead in his last years at the Board, just when world evangelization had broken through barriers in unprecedented ways.

Keith Parks prays with the Global Strategy Group, a group of top administrators of the Foreign Mission Board. (Photo courtesy, Sandy King, Baptist Press)

Following a luncheon in Rio de Janeiro, Brazil, in 1992, Southern Baptist missionaries Betty and Robert Gabriel express appreciation and bid farewell to Keith Parks for his years of service as Foreign Mission Board president. (Photo courtesy, Don Rutledge, Baptist Press)

Keith Parks chats with David Barrett, an Anglican missionary researcher and author whose assistance Parks enlisted for his 1980s global evangelization strategy. (Photo courtesy, Stanley Leary, SBC Foreign Mission Board)

Chapter 4

Double-Edged Crisis
for Parks and for Baptists

Keith lost his innocence about denominational politics in New Orleans.

—Helen Jean Parks

Two and one-half years into his FMB presidency, Parks first saw the fundamentalist handwriting on the wall. At the 1982 annual meeting of the Southern Baptist Convention, held in New Orleans, he received "the first inkling" that some day he might not be able to fulfill his calling through the Board. He remembered later thinking: "Their concern is not just with 'liberals.' They're not going to stop, even with conservatives like us."

"We were in a power struggle that we might lose." He said in retrospect, "They (the fundamentalists) didn't care about missions or church/state separation." He referred to a pro-Israel resolution being pushed by ultraconservative activists. Such a resolution, Parks felt, would endanger missionaries' lives and witness in parts of the Islamic world. Also, it would be a violation of the separation of church and state. Fundamentalists said they had received a fax from the White House urging the resolution's approval by the thousands of Southern Baptists participating at the annual meeting. Parks argued that this was even more reason not to pass the resolution. Why should Southern Baptists do the work of a government or of any political party?

He told Helen Jean: "We're in the hands of people who aren't real Southern Baptists." This conviction grew out of Parks' observation over several years. He believed the fundamentalists were ignoring basic Baptist precepts in their political attempt to take over the SBC. Although he had been optimistic in his first day as FMB president in January 1980, the tide had turned. The critical question was whether Southern Baptists in the pews would "understand what is at stake" in time to act. He began thinking it might already be too late. Helen Jean recalled later: "Keith lost his innocence about denominational politics at New Orleans." Until that meeting he had assumed calmer heads would prevail. People in the pews would immediately recognize the danger to their heritage, and they would stop this campaign.

What the Parks observed in 1982 was the fruit of fifteen years of fundamentalist dreaming and campaigning that had not really gone public in a major way until four years earlier. Judge Paul Pressler of Houston, Texas, and New Orleans Seminary student Paige Patterson, in a meeting now famous among Southern Baptists, talked until about 2 AM one night in 1967 at the Café du Monde in the same city where the 1982 Convention gave a wake-up call to traditional Southern Baptist leaders. It proved to be late into the 1970s before the ultraconservatives had marshaled sufficient forces to make their strength known. In another decade it was over. The fundamentalists had taken over the Southern Baptist Convention, electing the president each year and placing their loyalists on every board of every SBC agency, including the Foreign Mission Board, and dictating change in leadership and policies. Generations of trained leadership suddenly found their lives on unexpected tracks.

In correspondence as late as 28 May 1998, Parks deplored "the tragedy that has occurred in our convention when one group of Baptists can successfully intimidate, reward, punish, and control so many organizations." One agency president after another was pushed out of office. Parks fought the fundamentalist takeover for a decade as a denominational leader. "Following God's will," he often said, "doesn't mean pleasantness nor absence of grave difficulties, but those things aren't important in comparison." Even when the fight was lost, "the controversy" remained a part of his daily life throughout his CBF years. Baptist media accounts of the takeover's ongoing ramifications, along with phone calls and correspondence from a lifetime list of friends sharing the latest horror stories of careers wrecked and reputations ruined, all combined to keep the historic takeover's aftermath alive for him into the late 1990s.

Just as most Baptists were not aware of the specific difference Parks had already made in the recent history of Christian missions, little did they realize the effect the fundamentalist controversy would have on world evangelization. By forcing Parks out, the ultraconservative forces were taking away the one person who enabled the new-style, pioneer missionaries to work in their unorthodox ways in the so-called "closed" countries. (Instead of calling them "restricted-access" nations, Parks preferred to refer to them as countries requiring "creative access.") While some of the fundamentalists were truly excited about the work in World A, there was no guarantee Parks' successor would allow the program to continue to flourish. Traditional approaches might regain the upper hand again, with different administrators managing the pioneer work in ways that would inadvertently ruin its effectiveness.

With each passing year through the 1980s, Parks continued to speak out. He pulled no punches in deploring the tactics and the lack of concern displayed within the "ultraconservative resurgence" for what Parks considered to be a negative impact on missions. He publicly opposed the nomination of Charles Stanley as president of the Southern Baptist Convention. Stanley, pastor of First Baptist Church, Atlanta, Georgia, did not represent the cooperative missions model, as Parks saw it, because of the megachurch's

extensive, independent support for missionaries serving
with other mission agencies and what Parks thought to be
relatively small backing of SBC mission efforts. Electing
such leaders, who would then choose trustees to set policy
for the Board, would eventually erode the cooperative
missions model, he insisted.

He was traveling in West Africa when the trustees started
pushing for a special, called meeting of the Board to discuss
Parks' controversial statements about Stanley. The trustees
eventually agreed to wait for the next regular meeting of
trustees. Since fundamentalists weren't yet strong enough on
the board of trustees, they had to settle for a statement by
the majority affirming Parks' right to his opinion. From that
point forward Parks would be a constant target. Nevertheless he felt Baptists needed to know; this was the principle
that also led him to encourage Baptist journalists to "trust
the Lord and tell the people" the truth about what was happening to their denominational agencies. Baptist writers
awarded him a plaque for distinguished service as he retired
from the FMB in 1992 for his "commitment to honest and
open reporting."

North Carolina pastor Ed Beddingfield recalled a 1987
meeting in which he personally downplayed the Cooperative
Program in front of Parks because of fundamentalist efforts
to control the purse strings. He apologized to Parks
afterward. "No apology was necessary," Parks replied. "I
understood exactly what you meant." Beddingfield could see
that Parks was greatly upset by fundamentalist efforts to
control purse strings. (Beddingfield later proved instrumental in securing approval for CBF as a recognized faith group
for the endorsement of chaplains and pastoral counselors.)

Fundamentalists found it difficult to dislodge Parks
because his reputation as a Bible-believing missions leader
was unquestioned. "Never once was I accused of not

believing the Bible or of having liberal theology or of practicing poor missiology," he said. Ultraconservatives listened to him preach and then scratched their heads. "I don't understand how a man can preach like that—and not agree with us!"

"In earlier years," Parks told writer Robert O'Brien, "people were put on the FMB's board of trustees because of mission interest and commitment. In the 1980s the requirement was not commitment to missions, but to political takeover. Publicly and privately their rationale for decisions was not what was best for missions, but instead what those who appointed them wanted done."

"Support the conservative resurgence, and you can stay," Parks was told. This he refused to do. He would not attribute any characteristics to the Bible other than those its writers used to describe it. "The word 'inerrancy' is never used in the Bible," he noted repeatedly. To force every denominational employee to use certain descriptions for the Bible's inspiration went against all historic Baptist principles. Of Parks' stand Harlan Spurgeon recalled,

> During the final years at the Foreign Mission Board my appreciation for Dr. Parks grew steadily. I have never seen anyone endure such pressure and remain a joyful Christian. Dr. Parks' internal compass was true and unwavering. He faced hostile trustees six times per year and did so with true Christian grace. He knew who he was and Whose he was.
>
> He also knew who Baptists had been and should continue to be. At least a part of his secret was a small prayer group of which Joann and I were honored to be a part. God answered those prayers daily and filled Keith with God's Spirit.

Spurgeon said it caused him to fear for those who "worked day and night in an effort to remove [Parks] from the Foreign Mission Board."

Meanwhile the work abroad continued to bear fruit. During the Parks administration overseas baptisms and new church starts per annum doubled in less than ten years. In 1980 there were 110,032 baptisms reported overseas; by 1989, the number was 227,564. New churches per annum went from 11,510 to 21,242 by '89. The new methods being used by the Board's CSI administrative unit contributed to this increase among people groups previously yielding little if any fruit. During Parks' twelve years as president, the Board entered forty countries and numerous dependent territories. More than one hundred people groups were engaged by CSI in the last half of his tenure. Cooperative Program monies for the Board went from $34.4 million in 1980 to $69.1 million in 1992. The Lottie Moon Christmas Offering crowned his first year with a whopping $44.7 million, but that was little more than half the nearly $81 million garnered in 1992.

Parks knew the additional stakes at hand, the great opportunity for world evangelization being threatened by the ultraconservative takeover. This is what made the whole situation a double-edged crisis in Baptist life. After many years of struggle, however, he realized that continuing would be impossible.

By the spring of 1992 Parks no longer felt he could execute effectively the functions of the FMB presidency. Every move he made seemed to be questioned. Important decisions were postponed by trustees of the Board. "It was a grief experience," he said. "It was a loss." He sought in every possible way to gain a commitment from trustees to an unqualified support for FMB missionaries and their theology. Year after year he pleaded with the Convention, "Don't be sidetracked!" His battles with trustees in the later years at the Board showed that he had come a long way from earlier years when responsibilities and conflict made him ill. Indeed he was saddened by what was happening, but he fought ever harder against the tide. When all was said and done, in effect, he had helped lay the groundwork for a movement of Baptists in the South.

A bright young missions administrator on a visit to Richmond from his overseas post recalls a comment Parks made to him: "Maybe you can work with those guys [the fundamentalist trustees], but I can't." Parks was ready to resign and that spring announced he would technically "retire" at the end of October 1992.

It seemed fitting that his last trip abroad with the Board involved a July conference on global evangelization. Held in Rio de Janeiro, Brazil, the consultation built upon seven years of dialogue since the 1985 meeting Parks had convened at the Southern Baptist conference center in Ridgecrest, North Carolina. Those who knew the Americas said it was a milestone for increased engagement of Latin American Baptists. The three-day meeting drew missions leaders from three dozen nations. Parks was so persuasive in a speech concerning World A's needs, one of the Rio participants commented, "If Dr. Parks said there was a bus outside headed to Mongolia, I'd get on it." Longtime observers of the region believed missions had finally become first priority, thanks in part to Parks' efforts. The recipients were indeed becoming the givers of the gospel. The work had reached a new level.

A few months later Parks turned the reins of the Board over to interim president Don Kammerdiener. After many months of searching the Board elected Jerry Rankin to succeed Parks. As an area director whose region was affected by CSI work, Rankin had made no secret of his disagreement with CSI's position at the Board. In addition, he advocated a "harvest" philosophy that called for deployment of missionaries primarily to responsive peoples rather than in significant numbers to those believed to be resistant. Despite his desire to fold CSI work back into the traditional administrative structure, Rankin ended up giving the maverick group five years of frenetic expansion before abolishing its separate structure and reassigning all its 500-plus personnel to traditional administrative leadership. It would take years to sort out the ways for the ex-CSI missionaries to work within the old structures since their visas and new organizational names were geared toward secular ways of penetrating borders; the traditional missionaries operated openly as religious workers. Combining the two would jeopardize the hard-earned presence in a "closed" country.

In August 1990, two years before he announced his planned departure from the FMB, Parks attended an impromptu gathering of moderate Southern Baptists in Atlanta. A few hundred persons were expected to attend; 3,000 showed up. "It was a warm, spiritual moment," Parks recalled. "It was encouraging." The following year he attended another such meeting, as he eventually did every year. At that meeting trustees were aware in advance of his plans and strongly opposed his participation. He decided to go anyway. Bill Bruster, who later became CBF Network Coordinator, said Keith "was there as an observer at a meeting of Baptists, neither to bless nor to condemn." Parks, however, "paid a heavy price with FMB trustees for attending the meeting," Bruster noted.

In the May 1991 meeting in Atlanta, the name of the group was chosen. It would be called "the CBF," or Cooperative Baptist Fellowship. Missions was a strong focus of the organization from the beginning, Parks felt. That same year the Baptist seminary in Ruschlikon, Switzerland, was summarily "defunded" by the FMB trustees, a clear breach of the agency's promise to support the struggling European school over a long-term, phaseout plan. In a courageous commitment that also became a rallying cry, CBF pledged to "keep the promise."

In 1992 a total of ten missionary couples who resigned from the Board in protest over the trustees' European policies were offered CBF support. The first missionaries to break ties with the FMB were "T" and Kathie Thomas. Well-respected among European Baptists and popular guests in pulpits across the southeastern United States, the Thomases proved to be a rallying point for moderate Baptists ready to support missionaries resisting fundamentalist interference overseas. CBF pledged its support for each resigning missionary, and they went on the payroll in January 1993. The missionaires were:

- "T" and Kathie Thomas
- Jonlyn and Keith Parker
- JoAnn and John David Hopper
- Earl and Jane Martin
- John and Revonda Deal
- Margie and Paul Thibodeaux
- Becky and Jim Smith
- Debbie and Kent Blevins
- Joyce and Tom Cleary
- Jan and Kevin Rutledge

Meanwhile, Parks still had his call to missions, but had no means of exercising it. After announcing his retirement plans, he was given at the next CBF meeting "a standing ovation that lasted five or six minutes," Bruster recalled. The presence of Keith and Helen Jean "added a sense of legitimacy and electricity to the meeting."

In October 1992 the Parks family said farewell to Board staff and overseas field administrators who were in Richmond for consultations. The Parks' children flew to Virginia for the occasion. Keith appeared to be doing his best to keep his deep grief from showing too much, though it was evident. Hearts went out to him. Helen Jean continued to speak out, wanting the other side of the story to get a greater hearing among Southern Baptists.

"I left (the FMB) when I reached the point that I could not influence decisions for the good of missions," Parks shared later, "and could not lead foreign missions according to our Southern Baptist heritage of freedom and persuasion, rather than conformity and control." He prayed with Helen Jean about the future. He enjoyed the classroom but to return to teaching at that moment did not seem the right move. "There was never any question, never any desire to do anything but missions." A support group in Richmond talked with Keith and Helen Jean and prayed with them for a sense of direction.

"I decided to go back and read the book of Acts," Parks said in reconstructing that segment of his own journey. "As I came to the twentieth chapter, God seemed to be saying: 'I want you to notice this.' " It was the apostle Paul's farewell speech to the Ephesian elders during their rendezvous at Miletus (Acts 20:18ff.). Noting Paul's sense of the Spirit's leading, Parks recalled: "God was saying, 'You aren't finished.' It was an affirmation to continue somehow in global missions. 'Stay with it,' God seemed to be saying."

In November 1992, not long after he cleaned out his presidential desk, Keith and Helen Jean were asked to meet with the missions committee of CBF at a Catholic retreat center in Nashville. The couple prayed at length about the meeting. They had some specific ideas about what the Lord would have them to do with their remaining active years,

but did not know where that would lead. Also, Keith and
Helen Jean did not know what the committee had in mind.
Present at the committee meeting were:

• Jimmy Allen, a former president of the Southern Baptist
  Convention
• Jean Bond, a college professor in Mississippi and a former
  missionary
• Scott Walker, whose parents were missionaries and who is
  now pastor of First Baptist Church, Waco, Texas
• Alan Neely, a former missionary and professor
• Carolyn Weatherford Crumpler, a former director of
  Woman's Missionary Union
• Ben Loring, then pastor of First Baptist Church, Amarillo,
  Texas
• Peggy Pemble, a retired missionary from Brazil
• Edna Frances Dawkins, who was serving at the FMB when
  the Parks were appointed as missionaries
• Seth Macon, a member of First Baptist Church, Greens-
  boro, North Carolina
• Anne Neil, a former longtime missionary to West Africa

The Parks shared with the CBF committee what God
had laid on their hearts, even though they were unsure what
kind of reaction they would receive. Their intentions were
not to persuade but to make known what they themselves
must do. The vision was to do missions in a world without
borders, with no artificial dichotomy between home and
foreign missions. Unreached people groups would be the
major thrust, with an avoidance of institutional ministry in
general.

After the Parks had shared their convictions, the committee showed them a document written in previous
months. Many of its features outlined almost identical goals

to those Keith and Helen Jean expressed. "The Lord had led both the committee and us to the same basic focus," Parks said. The committee document became the mission statement that would lead CBF global missions for the next five years, followed by a slight revision in 1997 that set out the same broad emphases: World A, ministry to internationals (refugees, immigrants, students from abroad), inner-city ministry among the poor and abandoned, and service to Eastern Europe.

A new missions-sending body was born as part of a new Baptist movement, the Cooperative Baptist Fellowship. "It was a defining moment," said CBF Coordinator Daniel Vestal, in looking back to that earlier stage in the movement's brief history. "In some ways it was a legitimizing moment." Bob Allen of Associated Baptist Press wrote: "Keith Parks brought instant credibility to the Cooperative Baptist Fellowship."

Missionary "T" Thomas, who signed up with CBF just before Parks, said the highly respected leader "came with an ever-renewing vision for reaching the unreached." He noted that some of CBF's new missionaries later came "with 'old' ideas about how to do missions," while Parks "has been the 'young one' in his thinking." For Parks this newest adventure was simply God's will. "God had a better, more exciting, more fulfilling way than I could ever have imagined," Parks said to new missionaries later. "You can trust God." And God was now entrusting him with a major new work.

Chapter 5

Shaping a New Pioneer Outreach

I tell our missionaries that if they're not failing, they're not trying as many new things as they should. We've created a system that encourages experimentation and taking risks, and I think that's consistent with Christ's example.
—*Keith Parks*

Going from the frying pan into the fire might have been Keith Parks' thoughts when he got down to new business at the helm of CBF's embryonic missions program. This time it was not a case of fundamentalists, but of activists on the field, who joined in "combat" with the veteran missions executive.

The honeymoon before the first storm proved short-lived. Parks worked from his Richmond home in the first days of CBF employment in early 1993. Starting almost from scratch, he had for the first time in his forty-year career the opportunity to "do it right," without having to contend with entrenched traditions. His son Stan conducted most of the early research.

"The most fun is trying out new things," Parks shared with longtime friend Robert O'Brien, a Baptist journalist who left the FMB several years after Parks. "At the Fellowship we have the freedom to experiment, and if it doesn't work, to try something else. I tell our missionaries if they're not failing, they're not trying as many new things as they should."

In truth, his experience told him that new missionaries, in their first three or four years on the field, are fortunate if they learn the local language just well enough to do their work. (Often working with minorities, they would need the national language and the mother tongue of the particular ethnic group.) "My hope," he said half-joking, "is they come out, after the first term (the first three to four years), not having done more harm than good!" The second term and beyond are usually the most productive years. By then, MKs (missionaries' kids) consider the host country their real home. Their parents are comfortable in the language— although their accents offend their native-sounding children —and the family as a whole has become bicultural.

Part of Parks' vision was to create a mobile missionary force, unfettered by overseas institutions or real estate management. CBF missionaries would live in rental properties only, and they would arrive on the field with nothing more than they could check in excess baggage: No more embarrassing sights of Baptist missionary crates arriving in a Third World country, recreating an American "oasis" inside some colonial home on the hill. They would identify more with the local people, buying furniture and appliances in their host country. These were parts of Parks' ideal. He was pleased to see on his visits overseas and in the inner cities that quite a few CBF missionaries made the dream a reality.

Another element of Park's vision was to create a niche on the world missionary scene, not duplicating the effort of others or planting the CBF flag everywhere. CBF was too small to have such ambitions. "We can't be all things to all people," he reminded supporters. The objective would be to find the most neglected peoples, especially those in World A. If another mission agency were engaging a certain people group, CBF would keep on looking until it found a similar need overlooked by others.

Early conflict came from some of the missionaries who wanted to quit the FMB but stay right where they were under CBF's flag. Parks replied to such requests with a "no, thanks." CBF was not going to take "the controversy" to the mission field where national churches would be adversely affected more than ever. A transfer to another needy site would be the appropriate response.

The first ten missionary couples to go on the CBF payroll in January 1993 (one month before Parks) hoped to build a strong European ministry. The CBF Coordinating Council's Global Missions Ministry Group (GMMG) and the new CBF global missions coordinator, however, had other priorities. World A would be the principal arena, and field administrators would not be in the plan. Parks envisioned instead a flat administrative structure with self-managed field teams answering directly to an administrative team in Atlanta.

Later, when a missionary complained of having too little contact with Parks, he responded, half in jest: "Listen, the ones I talk to frequently are either having a problem, or I have a problem with them. Consider it a good thing if you don't hear from me!" CBF missionaries had to be self-starting, entrepreneurial types who could live with more ambiguity and less supervision.

In the European arena a number of CBF's first missionaries did not like what they were hearing. They thought CBF would want to work hand-in-hand with European Baptists in a vigorous new partnership, with the Europeans leading the way and the Americans committing themselves in a servant role to the Europeans' agendas. Unless strong support was given immediately, a golden opportunity would be lost in Europe, since the FMB was so unpopular there.

Parks discussed the new approach with the small missionary force he had inherited. The meeting was one of the toughest in his experience, with tempers flaring. He took the verbal blows with his trademark equanimity. The nervous stomach of his early years was long behind him. The avoidance of conflict was no longer a problem.

Parks separated the emotion on display from the persons manifesting it. The national-champion debating skills from his college days were still fresh, as were the decades of experience with strident critics in the United States. He adhered to his convictions and caused the European group to realize he wouldn't change his mind. Most stayed on board for the time being. Still, it would take years before the emotions would subside for some; even then their opinion would not have changed. In their minds Europe had lost to Asia and North Africa because of one person and the authority given him by some of CBF's top supporters in the US. Six years later, for various reasons not completely connected to Parks, only two CBF missionary couples still served in work chiefly tied to traditional European Baptist churches. Others continued on the continent, but they ministered among the persecuted Gypsies and the growing number of Muslim immigrants, or they resided in Europe as a base from which to itinerate into the Middle East and North Africa. Parks recalled later,

> Since then, less than ten percent [of CBF's missionaries] have come from the International Mission Board or the North American Mission Board. We require potential CBF missionaries to resign from the IMB or NAMB with no assurance of appointment. They can expect a change in assignment, which usually means a new language and a new culture.
>
> Candidates must demonstrate support for CBF's mission statement and our approach to missions, along with a commitment to learning how to function in this team environment.

The global missions team would foster a cooperative culture.

The field teams Parks planned to deploy needed to tackle neglected peoples of North Africa and Asia. CBF received invitations to participate with several European Baptist groups in a North African country and in Albania. Another invitation came from a bedouin in a Mideast nation who had dreamed he would partner someday with Christians in his homeland. At the time the FMB was working in that country, but it ministered with Baptist churches in Christian communities; CBF would work among the neglected, semi-nomadic Muslims through a humanitarian organization.

In the early days when Parks came on board with CBF, former FMB vice presidents Betty Law and Harlan Spurgeon joined the staff, too. Law dealt with administrative matters in general, making a significant contribution in developing a solid financial program, while Spurgeon developed the personnel selection process of the young missions program and assisted in early surveys and strategic development.

Grace Powell Freeman, a Georgian who had gone off to the Southern Baptist Theological Seminary in Louisville, Kentucky, and later to New York for marriage and ministry, returned to her native state and joined Parks in September 1994. She led missions education and promotion efforts with an attention to detail that was sorely needed. She loved the missionaries and displayed a pastoral touch that proved indispensable.

She was joined in February 1995 by Tom Prevost, a former home missionary and later an FMB personnel administrator who came to CBF from the Virginia Baptist missions department. He developed CBF mission partnerships, codified the growing number of polices and procedures necessary for the multiplying missionary force, and closely monitored the budgeting process. At first Parks resisted a book of guidelines, preferring a more unfettered missions force and remembering how such matters had slowed down change in previous eras. He would say to some new situation at CBF, "We have no policy," and would be comfortable with the ambiguity. Prevost responded to Parks, "Yes, we do have a policy. It's in your head! We need it on paper!" By the time Parks retired, the guidelines for field personnel had grown to more than sixty pages. That was one battle he lost.

How was CBF viewed by those outside the staff? Baptist missiologist Alan Neely, in a 1998 comparison of various Baptist missions programs, judged CBF as having a more global view than other agencies, referring to its motto of "Doing Missions in a World without Borders"—which focused on removing the usual dichotomy between overseas and home missions. Seeing CBF as manifesting "something new and fresh," he found it "far more open to different kinds of Southern Baptists than is the IMB."

Parks and his staff, with the approval of the CBF Coordinating Council's Global Missions Ministry Group (GMMG), on occasion affirmed for appointment some missionary candidates who were previously divorced. In addition, although most CBF missionaries are conservative in their doctrinal orientation, they show evidence of being tolerant of less rigid views, Neely observed. Women are affirmed in ministry to any calling for which God has provided the spiritual gifts. A number of laypersons are appointed for CBF service if they have marketable skills vital in gaining a visa to some locales.

Nevertheless Neely noted the weaknesses of the CBF approach, primarily its dependence "on the gifts of a relatively small number of churches and individuals. The level of funding for missions by the CBF is substantial," Neely observed, "but unless the number of supporting churches grows steadily, the current level is not likely to increase significantly." By November 1998 the number of churches giving to CBF had surpassed 1,700. In that year ninety-eight additional churches in Texas joined the movement, which called itself "a new way to be Baptist." A blitz of the state earlier in the year had Parks, Vestal, and other CBF leaders criss-crossing Texas, speaking to pastors and church activists who wanted to learn more about the Fellowship.

The need to expand the movement's base of local church support drove Parks more than ever before—at the age most have retired to their gardens and golf—to travel America with his new global missions message for CBF. Almost every Sunday morning, and frequently on Sunday and Wednesday evenings for six years with CBF, he could be seen in a Baptist pulpit, somewhere between West Texas and Richmond, Virginia. His messages were sharp and clear—except for the one occasion when a misread prescription drug dosage caused him to preach a rambling, repetitive message twice as long as the norm and not to remember what he had said! Saturday evenings, Sunday evenings, or Monday mornings found him on an airplane, scrunched in the economy class and nursing a bum knee, trying to find something worth reading from the airline's magazine. (He loved to read Louis L'Amour westerns for many years and in later years was always searching for something new to read.)

When he could drive to a speaking engagement, fellow motorists might very well see him holding a dictaphone near his mouth with one hand while steering with the other. ("I am a safe driver!" he insisted.) His in-box for correspondence almost always required a reply. Each season also brought its share of week-long campaigns throughout a given state, a blitz of churches wanting to hear more about CBF. Scores of wealthy Baptists, along with the not-so-wealthy, lined up their estate planning to include CBF in their wills because of Keith Parks. On overseas trips his pace exhausted younger men. Jet lag seemed to have little effect. At home he seldom retired for the night before 11:30, feeding his news addiction by watching television or surfing the Internet or reading e-mail from family and friends.

Harlan Spurgeon, an administrator under Parks at the FMB and at CBF, called Parks' physical stamina "legendary." He said, "I have never been able to understand how he could work harder than anyone through the week and then travel across the nation to speak in some far off church on missions. The following Monday he was back in the office looking fresher than those twenty years his junior." (That last phrase might be the legendary part.) Spurgeon recalled,

> He is a delightful traveling companion. He has a wry sense of humor and can see the funny side in every kind of situation. He also has a cast-iron stomach. On a trip to India to check on the land of origin of the Gypsy people, I became weak and dehydrated from something I ate. Keith never missed a meal, eating everything in sight. He almost had to carry me on board the plane when it came time to depart.

From the pew Parks was seen as outgoing and comfortable with a crowd, desiring to share as long as time allowed. Indeed he was a gifted teacher, his most joyful moments coming when, to illustrate a sermon, he entered fully into the telling of stories from his own missionary career, reliving for a few minutes the best memories of a memorable life. In reality he was introverted and enjoyed his brief moments alone on the road or at home with Helen Jean in a wooded subdivision just north of Atlanta's Perimeter. They practiced a simple lifestyle, as a committed Christian witness and as a means of providing more financially for missions.

After he came to CBF, Parks refused a generous salary, strongly favored by founding CBF Coordinator Cecil Sherman, that would have paid him per annum $20,000 to $35,000 more than a senior missionary having decades of experience. Instead, he won approval for all CBF global missions administrative staff to be paid on the missionary scale. "I want staff coming on board for the right motivation," he said, wanting also to send the right message to missionaries about home office personnel. So conscientious was he about avoiding any appearance of luxury that a black stretch limousine arranged in Louisiana by a FMB trustee greatly embarrassed him on his first trip as president in 1980. He tried to avoid any prospect of repeat performances anywhere thereafter, both at the FMB and at the CBF.

At the end of his career he still fought that battle. Writing 23 November 1998, to the committee seeking his successor, Parks urged the group "to avoid the temptation to pay someone to take this job." He explained,

> I am convinced that if financial motivation has to be added in order to cause a person to accept this responsibility, it will create at the least an awkwardness, if not an embarrassment, when the realization comes that there are doctors and engineers and other successful professionals who took considerably less money because of their calling to go to the mission field and who are living in circumstances much more difficult than [those of] Atlanta. I think it erodes the credibility and the confidence of missions leadership if the person accepting the responsibility has to be motivated financially to do so.

This statement spoke of Parks' way of life. Every aspect of his being seemed to revolve around missions. Among his favorite Bible passages are Romans 15, Ephesians 3, and John 1—all of which speak to the heartbeat of a missionary God, a missionary Son, and a missionary apostle. Keith and Helen Jean were married as much to global missions as to each other. Indeed they were "parents" to a global missions family as much as to their own four children. Parks had a love and gift for dealing with children. Carol Prevost, whose husband, Tom, served on staff at the Foreign Mission Board in Richmond, Virginia, and later at CBF in Atlanta, remembers how Parks, in a crowd of adults, would "zero in" on children, showing genuine interest. "T" Thomas noted this personal involvement, too, at the European Baptist Congress in Lillehammar, Norway. While other top leaders talked among themselves, Parks enjoyed playing with the children and expressing "his Christlike love for all people—young or old, reached or unreached."

The Parks children also emulate a simple Christian lifestyle of Great Commission commitment. All four have been in the ministry. The three sons live overseas: Randall with his family in Cairo, and Kent and Stan with theirs in Southeast Asia. Eloise serves as a chaplain to AIDS patients in the Dallas-Fort Worth metroplex, where Keith and Helen Jean planned to resettle in June 1998.

Before resting from his round-the-clock ministry, Parks witnessed a phenomenal growth in missionary deployment at CBF. Exactly three years after he became Global Missions Coordinator, he found that the number of CBF missionaries had increased five-fold, from the original twenty of Europe to one hundred on three continents (eighty career or long-term, twenty serving for two years in the Global Service Corps). By June 1997 the CBF had reached an all-time high of 151 missionaries. In four and a half years the Fellowship had assembled a missionary force larger than most sending groups a century old. True, the mammoth IMB and a few other organizations such as Youth with a Mission (YWAM) deployed thousands, but most missionary societies of sending nations are very small groups with a few dozen missionaries. CBF's achievement was astounding for a new movement not even in its "teen years."

The CBF missions administrative staff grew much more slowly than the field forces. After Betty Law, who retired in

1995, and Harlan Spurgeon, who retired in 1996, came first Grace Powell Freeman and later Tom Prevost, with Flint Miller and Gary Baldridge joining the staff in the spring of 1996. Another staff member for mission finance was to be added in early 1999 just as Parks was retiring. Freeman, a native of Newnan, Georgia, who had worked with the American Bible Society in New York City, brought a greatly needed attention to detail and an appreciation for the formidable challenges of U.S. urban missions. Prevost, a former U.S. missionary in various Western states, contributed among other things an intricate knowledge of Baptist state organizations from his Virginia years and a grasp of personnel selection from FMB staff service. Miller, who served as a journeyman in South Korea, had oriented and debriefed short-term personnel for the FMB. Baldridge, a missionary with the FMB for seventeen years, was trained with his wife Barbara in the first group of new NRMs to World A after the Smiths and Stroopes made their prototype debuts. In addition to these Atlanta administrators, Parks farmed out other staff functions to some of the CBF missionaries working elsewhere in North America.

The loss of Spurgeon to retirement proved to be a personal disappointment for both the Parks and the couple from Missouri. "Joann and I consider the friendship we have enjoyed with Keith and Helen Jean Parks as a personal treasure," Spurgeon said. Whether in Richmond with the FMB or in Atlanta with the (CBF) Global Missions Office, both couples enjoyed impromptu dinner dates. The only problem was that a pattern developed. "We would find a restaurant that we especially liked and before long, the restaurant would close. Now that we are retired to Missouri we often ask each other on the phone, 'Have you closed any good restaurants lately?'"

The way Parks filled those staff slots said a lot about him. He once made a 1600-mile round trip in one day to spend seven hours with a prospective staff member, giving the entire time to that candidate and his family. He did not take or make a single telephone call during the visit, nor did he check e-mail on a portable computer the way most busy executives do. Rather, he focused on finding the right person with World A experience for his staff to help maintain the strategic priority in the years beyond his own departure from the scene. Of Parks' commitment to finding the right person for a given job, Harlan Spurgeon noted:

> Keith is an excellent student of human nature. When he meets with someone, he makes him feel as if he is the only person on earth. But he soon knows what makes them tick. After a while Keith knew that I was an ESTJ on the Myers-Briggs inventory who really liked to cut the talk and get things done. I wanted decisions and wanted them right now. Keith learned that he could hold out awhile and that I would become frustrated and accept anything so long as it represented a decision. This became a humorous inside joke with us, but was very true.

Growing numbers of field personnel and a slightly expanding staff were made possible by big increases in giving from the churches. Monthly contributions climbed from $333,399 in July 1991 to an all-time high of $2,368,172 in January 1998. The Global Missions Offering reached $4,453,842 in the 1997-1998 fiscal year and appeared headed for a 12.55% increase in 1998-1999.

As field staff mushroomed, Parks knew he soon would have to put into place some form of field administration. He hoped to avoid a layer of administration between field personnel and the home office. Some form of semiautonomous team management was the way he wanted to go. He prayed for guidance. "Old hierarchical models based on centralized control and top-down decision making," he wrote in the CBF monthly newsletter, "are inconsistent with the vision that gave birth to the Fellowship."

In a message to First Baptist Church in Athens, Georgia, Parks described his dream of a self-managed missionary force. After the service Patty Brantley approached him and said, "You talked about team training. That's what my husband does." Parks responded, "Your husband is the man I'm looking for. I just didn't know his name."

It turned out that John Brantley had first offered these very same services to various Baptist organizations years ago, but none had taken him up on the offer. He took his skills to industry, and companies responded enthusiastically. A former pastor trained at Southern Baptist Seminary in Louisville, Kentucky, Brantley longed to take these skills into churches and Christian organizations. The two men had a deal.

Brantley took his enthusiasm and outgoing personality to CBF missionaries in Asia, Europe, and North America, after first training CBF's global missions staff. He led the staff to articulate its vision, mission, and goals. An eighteen-month process began. Virtually all CBF missions personnel participated in the numerous drafts of a document setting out the decision-making process within the organization. Most decisions were to be made on the mission field by teams working together toward consensus. Staff were assigned as coaches to each of the twelve field teams or clusters. Parks and Brantley sought to cultivate a cooperative culture; "lone rangers" need not apply.

This cooperation extended beyond those employed by CBF to Great Commission Christians of all denominations and nationalities. CBF missionaries sought to work in tandem with any agency or organization that would cooperate with them. By the time Parks left his Atlanta office, more than 90 percent of CBF's career missionaries gave at least a portion of their energies to cooperative efforts among the more unevangelized peoples of Asia and North Africa and among their immigrants and refugees scattered across Europe and the United States. For the majority, this work was full-time. Others played support roles to both World A and other endeavors or gave part of their time to World A's diaspora in Worlds B and C.

CBF missionaries worked among eight major ethno-linguistic families in the Eastern Hemisphere:

- Afro-Asiatic: principally in North Africa and the Middle East
- Altaic: the Turkic peoples of Central Asia and Turkey
- Austro-Asiatic: mainly in Indochina
- Austronesian: mostly in Indonesia, Malaysia, and southern Thailand
- Daic: Thailand and beyond
- Indo-European: Albanians, Kurds, Iranians, Gypsies
- North Caucasian: mountain peoples on Russia's southwest border
- Sino-Tibetan: principally in China

These World A missionaries were supported by technical field staff for electronic communications and by a team working in the diplomatic communities of Brussels, New York, and Washington. In addition, other CBF missionaries in Europe and North America contributed part or all of their ministry time to immigrants, refugees, or students from World A in Brussels, Toronto, Vancouver, Dearborn, Los Angeles, New York, and Boston.

Besides work among the unevangelized, CBF addressed inner city needs in Miami, New York City, and St. Louis, ministering to AIDS patients, the homeless, and others among the poorest of the poor. In Atlanta some of these ministries were also to be found among the work of CBF missionaries, in addition to their service to World A immigrants and refugees there. For a few years CBF missionaries supplied the leadership to Youth Missions Exchange in Louisville and also coordinated volunteer needs. In Europe, CBF related to the European Baptist Federation, the International Baptist Theological Seminary (IBTS) in Prague, and ESL ministries (teaching English as a second language) in the Czech Republic and Poland.

The IBTS board of trustees voted in 1997 to turn the seminary away from a traditional, residential center in competition with other European schools and toward a new, uncertain future as a specialized training point geared to meet specific, short-term needs unaddressed by other institutions across the continent. Parks interpreted these events in a positive vein, although students, faculty, and some long-time supporters saw the move differently. He wrote to the CBF Coordinating Council's Global Missions Ministry Group (GMMG),

> I hope we can keep a balanced perspective and keep uppermost in our awareness the fact that the European Baptists do, in fact, own the institution and had every right to make the decision they made the way they made it.
>
> Hopefully, this will create a European identification and ownership that has not materialized before now. Hopefully, it will, in fact, strengthen theological education throughout the forty-five theological institutions that have risen up in Europe in these last few years. I hope we can affirm them in the right to make the decision even if some would disagree with the decision they made.

Many did disagree. Faculty members, including two CBF missionary couples, did not quite see it the way Parks viewed it. Some felt betrayed. Nevertheless the changes came. By the summer of 1998 CBF no longer deployed personnel to IBTS. Funding continued, however, on a declining scale with annual grants included in the CBF global missions budget. CBF missionary Jim Smith, the Fellowship's liaison to the European Baptist Federation, remained a vital member of the IBTS board.

The support Parks gave to the principle of overseas Baptists making their own decisions and taking responsibility for the work was consistent with his view on indigenous church planting. He often contended with missionaries who wanted to pay pastors' or evangelists' salaries in an open-ended, indefinite way. "If we create an attitude that there cannot be church planting without foreign funds . . . we are going to limit planting of churches. We must move toward the local resources providing the support." Such was the way for longstanding church growth, he believed.

"These are stimulating and challenging days to be involved in CBF's Global Missions Program," Park reported to CBF's Global Missions Ministry Group (GMMG) in October 1997. He cited new developments "taking a good bit of creativity, energy, and time. These would include the envoy program, chaplaincy program, and the possibility of Global Service Corps (GSC) bringing its own support." Tom Prevost, who had led a steadily growing volunteer force to reach 3,500 participants each year, instituted an envoy program to harness the potential of Baptists and others serving with corporations or on institutional contracts abroad. Parks' team also had gained responsibility for endorsing chaplains, pastoral counselors, and other ministers in specialized settings. Missionaries serving more than one month and less than three years with the GSC would soon start raising their own support (despite some misgivings within the GMMG). Career missionaries would continue under the long-established system of pooled resources from churches' designated gifts and mission offerings.

The influence of CBF missionaries proved to be much greater than their numbers because most field personnel were catalytic. They facilitated the work of still larger numbers of workers from many denominations and nationalities. Some have produced results far beyond the needs of one people group. (Safeguards required to avoid jeopardizing the work preclude identification of the missionaries by name.) They proved instrumental in the historic creation and development of a nationwide network of Asian Christians who committed themselves to identify, prioritize, and engage every unreached people group in a particular Asian nation. The remaining unevangelized people groups in that country have been informally classified into clusters having several people groups each. By 1998 facilitators were recruited for all the clusters. For the first time in history this Southeast Asian nation's evangelical leaders from many denominations will address spiritual needs of every neglected people group in the country, no matter how remote.

Another CBF SC unit, Beth and Tom Ogburn, combined their considerable spiritual gifts and talents to bring together for the first time various mission agencies that had worked independently for decades among an apparently unresponsive people group spread across several Asian nations. Their efforts led to the development of a resource center shared by all and an annual consultation making strides toward eventual evangelization of the Muslim people on which they focused. More important, daily and weekly contact started taking place between workers of various Christian organizations. As a result, they all avoided duplication of effort and also combined their resources to move projects to fulfillment in record time. (Descriptions here are somewhat vague for security reasons. Muslim monitors try to detect such work and to shut it down.)

Following is one example of how this cooperation works: Four missionaries (three Americans from three different mission agencies and one former pastor born in the host country) sat down to lunch in an Asian capital in November 1998. A fifth person at the table was another national of the host country who had been trained by Wycliffe Bible Translators. Within an hour the group agreed on a plan that would give that nation's majority people group a contextualized version of the New Testament in little more than three years. Two previous attempts had failed. This one would succeed, however, because of advocates who were full-time strategy coordinators.

In his last summer as head of CBF's global missions work, Parks gave a devotional to staff members from Exodus 3, where God commissioned Moses to lead the Israelites out of Egypt. "Nearly every time," Parks said, "the way God does something is by sending someone. God hears, sees, has concern, and when it comes to doing something about it, God looks for a faithful servant and says, 'I am sending you.'"

Parks continued in that vein to share with CBF staff outside the global missions office (those working in finance and other administrative offices) some of the annual reports recently received from the field, from those "sent ones" for whom everyone had been praying. Following are some of those reports:

• Sam and Latha Bandela formed a strategic interdenominational partnership with thirty-five churches in developing the Chamblee-Doraville Ministry Center on Atlanta's northern edge.

- Nomie Derani, "under the watchful eye of the religious leaders of the Arab-American community" in the Midwest, helped train dozens of youth for the teams of four mission agencies.

- Fran and Lonnie Turner made significant contact with representatives of eighty-two nations in their work related to the diplomatic community of Brussels, Belgium.

- Some Arabs from a country where missionaries were prohibited said their hearts were "sick" and came from a far distance to see a CBF nurse in another Middle East nation. They sought copies of the New Testament in Arabic and videos on the life of Jesus, with the voices dubbed in Arabic. They planned to duplicate and share these materials from oasis to oasis.

- CBF-sponsored Wycliffe translators, Kirk and Suzie Person, recorded the last words of an AIDS victim in Thailand who said of the gospel, "It's too late for me."

Parks could have continued for hours describing the doors God had opened, just as the apostle Paul must have done when he returned on his first missionary "furlough" to Antioch (Acts 14:27). He could have told about China and how the CBF had committed itself to a "one-track approach" there. This meant that its representatives pledged to work openly with the China Christian Council and to abstain from any attempts at clandestine ministry. Parks' deliberate strategy was to cooperate fully with the government-recognized churches, hoping thereby to find ample opportunity for outreach to the most neglected of China's minority ethnic groups, or "nationalities," as the Chinese called them.

Parks' approach caused a clash with the SBC's International Mission Board, which accused CBF of influencing the Chinese government's decision to disassociate itself from IMB workers. Parks vehemently denied the accusation in extensive statements released to the press. He and IMB President Jerry Rankin had discussed these matters before.

To Parks, in general, the IMB seemed to be deliberately avoiding cooperation with CBF. He said he was told by more than one IMB leader that there could be no formal cooperation as long as the Fellowship refused to declare itself as a separate denomination. CBF had already voted down that very suggestion. Meanwhile on the mission field a fair number of IMB missionaries and some of their regional leaders worked informally with CBF missionaries on various projects. The CBF stance was to cooperate with every organization willing to do so.

Indeed one of the last major initiatives of Parks' administration was to beef up the interagency mobilization efforts for World A. In the autumn of 1996 CBF's missionaries to World A had been invited to Atlanta for consultations. Two of the principal recommendations from those meetings were for staff to encourage CBF-related churches to "adopt" people groups in World A and to find additional missionaries whose chief assignment would be to mobilize the worldwide church in behalf of World A needs. These mobilizers would be assigned to specific "christianized" regions of the world from which they would bring resources to bear upon the needs of unevangelized peoples in North Africa and parts of Asia. In February 1999 CBF missionaries Beth and Tom Ogburn were selected to transfer to one of these roles, combining the "Adopt-a-People" coordination with the continued emphases on prayer and North American mobilization of other Great Commission Christian groups.

Meanwhile, mobilizers were slated for appointment to Africa and Latin America.

At the same time one of CBF's global mission partners, strategy-coordination trainer Eric Watt of Virginia Beach, Virginia, established in late 1998 a new organization called the Network for Strategic Mission. With Watt's ties to some of the most effective networks in global missions, he sought to lay the groundwork for connecting these resources at strategic points and moments well into the next century of frontier missions. He asked for two CBF strategy coordinators to be seconded to this new enterprise, leading the regions of Middle East and North Africa and Southeast Asia. CBF agreed. Jerry and Lorraine McAtee and Erika and Kent Parks were set apart for this new venture. As a result CBF would be an increasingly vital part of what other Great Commission Christians planned in cooperative efforts for the twenty-first century.

With these and many other initiatives well under way, Parks believed he should turn the coordination over to new leadership in CBF global missons. Early in the summer of 1998, Parks told CBF Coordinator Daniel Vestal, who had succeeded Cecil Sherman, that he would retire at the end of February 1999, six years and one month after his first day as Global Missions Coordinator of CBF. The Fellowship's Coordinating Council would meet in late February, and Parks hoped to say his farewell at that time.

"It just felt like the time has come," Parks explained in the announcement on 18 September. "I have no health problems, and nobody's asking me to leave." In fact, in October 1997 the Personnel Committee recommended continuation beyond "the twentieth anniversary of Keith's fiftieth birthday," as Chairman Welton Gaddy phrased it. Not a single word of opposition to Parks' continuation came to the floor of the CBF Coordinating Council's meeting.

Parks would be under annual review from that moment forward, as would any employee who turned seventy. (He had excused himself from the Council meeting during the discussion; no one told him when it was over. Waiting for quite awhile outside, he wondered if he still had a job!) A number of months later, Vestal urged Parks to be in no rush about leaving; the Fellowship's officers would leave the timing to him. "I did have some fear," Parks admitted, "about staying beyond the time I was productive." He and Helen Jean continued to pray for guidance.

That fear proved unfounded for Keith, but a freak occurrence did slow down Helen Jean. Not long after the venerable couple made their still-secret decision to announce later their retirement plans, Helen Jean fell while walking with Keith in their Atlanta neighborhood one Saturday evening in late July 1998. The fall fractured her jaw. Recovery took twice the length of time expected. In an e-mail message to friends dated August 1, Helen Jean wrote

> The nurses at Northside Hospital said the personnel director wanted to talk to Keith about hiring him! He is absolutely the best. Nobody could be more thoughtful, helpful, humorous in bad situations, tough when he needs to be. [He's the] all-around best servant Christian I believe I know. My only complaint is that he makes me feel guilty because he does so much for me, and it keeps him from doing other things he needs to do.

Parks could not help but wonder if some unforeseen mishap or illness might befall him also; he, of course, wanted to be fully productive until his CBF successor was named. Although there were the inevitable private grumbles in the last year or two from some of CBF's most active church leaders who were impatient for change, all the Fellowship's constituents knew that Parks' productivity never waned. He provided credibility, fund-raising skills, and stability to the young missions program.

A confirmation for Parks of the "oughtness" regarding his retirement plans came when he realized certain needed steps in the advancement of CBF would not take place until his successor was named. Other CBF leaders were postponing new measures within staff, he said, waiting for their new team member, the next global missions coordinator, to join them. Parks did not want to stand in the way of progress on any front.

After informing CBF Coordinator Daniel Vestal of his decision to retire in February 1999, Parks quickly moved to share the decision with his children and staff. His greatest concern was that his family and staff would hear it from someone else. He hated surprises and assumed rightly that those close to him in this case would, too.

As administrative staff who were assembled in the conference room of CBF's offices on Mercer University's Atlanta campus started to express themselves emotionally over the momentous decision, Parks put up his hand and said, "I don't want to get sentimental now." One staff member said of Parks' departure date: "That will be a sad day." "Yes, well," Parks responded, "I'll miss you guys."

To the CBF Advisory Council in September 1998 and to the Coordinating Council in October, Parks outlined some of the challenges that lay before them in the future of CBF global missions. These challenges included:

• maintaining and strengthening the team approach to missions
• providing sufficient financial support for missions
• upholding the career category for missionary personnel
• maintaining the distinctiveness of CBF's missions program
• communicating the missions challenge to churches

- maintaining priorities and strategies
- maintaining security for overseas personnel while also informing constituents

"These challenges," Parks concluded, "sound like fun, which I hate to miss. But the Lord's timing is clear, and I am confident that the future of global missions and CBF will flourish under His leadership."

Agreeing to continue briefly in Atlanta beyond February 1999, Parks would be available part-time to speak in churches, help with a new endowment campaign, and advise staff if the search committee needed a bit more time. His global missions administrative associates would handle daily business as a team until then, with Parks retaining leadership in title part-time. He and Helen Jean would take their time in moving to the Dallas-Fort Worth area. "I've moved Helen Jean quickly too many times," he said.

Once settled in Texas, approaching his 72nd birthday, Parks planned to "get some things down on paper" with the help of Helen Jean who had studied journalism in college; had worked for a time as a writer for the daily Abilene (Texas) *Reporter-News*; and had written a book in the early 1980s on intercessory prayer for missions, *Holding the Ropes*. Keith had resisted the temptation to give much time to writing until retirement. There were too many other matters pressing for attention; he "didn't feel right" about giving significant time to anything other than the main thing—world evangelization.

On 2 December 1998 at 9:13 PM, good news arrived from United Nations headquarters in New York City. A member of CBF's team of representatives to the diplomatic community, David D'Amico, announced the next morning to Parks and to the entire Fellowship's community that the UN had granted accreditation to CBF as a nongovernmental organization. This granting of "associative status," D'Amico explained, would "open many more doors for us here and assist our colleagues around the world." It was a fitting Christmas gift for Parks in his last holiday season at CBF. The Fellowship's global missions program had indeed become a useful tool in God's hands for honorable work (2 Tim 2:21).

Keith Parks and Daniel Vestal share an embrace during Parks' tenure as CBF Global Missions Coordinator. (Photo courtesy, Fred Prosser)

Chapter 6

The Legacy of Keith Parks

It is extremely important that the person assuming this responsibility have a passion for "World A" and the unreached people groups . . . I cannot exaggerate how difficult it is to maintain the emphasis on unreached peoples when you are constantly bombarded with the worthwhile needy mission projects and mission emphases that are being promoted by your best friends and sometimes your strongest supporters.
—Keith Parks

In a career filled with accolades Parks received honorary doctorates from five universities—Hardin-Simmons, California Baptist, Southwest Baptist, University of Richmond and Mercer—distinguished alumnus awards from North Texas State University and Southwestern Seminary, denominational and citizenship awards for distinguished service, and numerous other national and international citations for distinguished service. His greatest honor, however, was serving as a missionary, which was made evident later in life every time he gave a verbal illustration from his Indonesian experience.

Indeed there are joys in the missionary life that go unsurpassed. Nothing can be more fulfilling than to be effective while being clearly obedient to the biblical command to make Christian disciples of all peoples. Of the work he left behind at CBF, Parks said, "I've seen a lot of evidence that the kind of missions effort we've shaped has the blessing of the Lord and is consistent with trends in society. Those elements will cause it to continue to grow." What constitutes his legacy?

First, his life provides quite a bit worthy of emulation. The manner in which Parks overcame serious illness at a young age and debilitating nervousness when given responsibility can provide encouragement to those facing similar obstacles. Then, he showed that it's never too late to seek help and to learn how to deal with conflict in a constructive way, both in one's marriage and ministry. His humble, servant spirit won followers. One day in the Atlanta office of CBF, a "street minister" showed up unannounced, wanting to speak to someone about missions. While other staff members wondered whether or not to interrupt their tasks at hand, Parks did not hesitate to walk across the building to the reception area, meet the young man, escort him to his office, and give him a hearing.

"Jesus picked up a towel, not a Torah," he told new missionaries in his traditional charge at the commissioning service in Louisville, Kentucky, in June 1997. "The people of the world will be impacted more when you pick up your towel and get down on your knees."

Parks set the pace for others in terms of a simple lifestyle, refusing a six-figure salary (or anything close to it) in order to save more resources for missions and to identify more with the missionary pay scale. When pay raises were forced upon him, he just gave more to the missions offering, according to one Richmond source, who added that sometimes his was probably the largest single gift from a particular church.

His missionary methods in Indonesia gave others a model to follow in personal ministry and in church growth. The Parks' children followed in their parents' footsteps, performing admirable, highly effective ministry. His only daughter, Eloise Parks, said, "If Dad told me the sky is purple, I wouldn't even walk to the window to see. That's how honest he's always been with us." In addition, his willingness to give up control and to delegate decisions to field personnel spoke volumes about his trust in missionaries. Robert O'Brien cited his integrity and his conviction that "Baptists need to know" the truth about their denomination's doings.

It was for this that Baptist media leaders awarded him their citation for distinguished service in 1992.

Tom Prevost of the CBF staff Parks' love for the career missionary as a secret of his power as a leader. An example: "I am deeply burdened for you and the children," Parks once wrote to a troubled young couple. "I regret that my schedule is rushed right now. I am traveling. My hope is to call you. I am praying that you will continue to pray about coming home sooner. We would like to provide some support to your family to go for some assistance in resolving your difficulties. I recognize that you may resent this as an intrusion. I pray you will receive it as a concern and a burden of a Christian brother."

His example regarding the priority of prayer made intercessory networks an essential piece in all future Baptist strategies. "Neither I nor the four children ever remember Keith not having his devotional time early in the morning," Helen Jean recalled. He loved to tell churches that "the most commonly stated need missionaries expressed beyond all others" was prayer support. "I've come to the conviction that the only thing which will touch unreached people groups is prayer." Almost all of CBF's new missionaries from 1993 to 1996 regretted that they had not taken more time at the beginning of their ministry to enlist an extensive network of committed prayer partners. From then on, new missionaries were given more time among CBF churches before they departed for their fields of service.

This prayer emphasis grew partly out of Parks' encounters with Chinese Christians who had suffered through the Cultural Revolution. They told him of how much Psalm 23 and 2 Corinthians 1 had comforted them. "They would get emotional about hearing on the radio that other Christians in other countries were praying for them," Parks said. He encouraged new missionaries to realize how dependent they would be on the Lord and on Christians praying for them.

When Parks preached, he spoke his convictions. He really believed God would reconcile all creation someday in Christ. He loved to open a dog-eared Bible—Eugene H. Peterson's *The Message* being one of his favorite versions—with new missionaries, laying out the great mystery of the ages from Ephesians 1 and 3 or Colossians 1. Parks also believed with all his heart in the uniqueness of Christ, quoting John 1:1-14, one of his favorite passages, and John 14:6 and Acts 4:12. His convictions also meant that he could not compromise his principles, especially with intolerant fundamentalists. By standing up against them, he also gave CBF instant credibility among the older generation of Southern Baptists and helped encourage the financial giving that laid a strong foundation for CBF's future. Because he believed so strongly, he became what today is a rare example of one who gives his life completely to a worthy cause. His vocation was also his avocation; round the clock there was seldom an hour when missions did not occupy his thoughts. The results of that dedication are obvious today.

When one lives out convictions in life, a prophetic gift seems a natural outgrowth, as if the Spirit awards obedience with a burden to preach. And preach Parks did. He has probably spoken in person to as many Baptist congregations as anyone in history. Parks sometimes used these Wednesdays and Sundays and special days to speak out about U.S. materialism and always to share missions opportunities that should be seized.

"Materialism," he told Baptists across the South, "is of greater value in the U.S. these days than spirituality." He was "distressed," for example, at how much time, money, and energy went into commercialized spirituality and Christmas celebrations. "When it's all said and done, what have we done to reveal God? The story of the birth of Christ is an evangelistic story." He loved the celebrations among first- and second-generation Christians in Indonesia. There, Christmas was celebrated by Asian Christians "as theological discussions and church," not as private families. Believers who had come to Christ in the previous year gave testimony. It was also an opportunity for evangelistic meetings.

He saw America's lack of interest in the rest of the world as selfishness. When prominent church leaders wanted to dilute the centrality of missions at national gatherings, Parks went toe-to-toe with them. He fought the tendency to equate all ministry with missions. Being a practical man, he also knew that missions paid the bill for a lot of other endeavors in denominational activities. He usually won his arguments when the bread-and-butter issue surfaced. Contributions depended on a missions emphasis.

Few missions leaders in the history of Christianity have seen more money flow into the cause than Keith Parks. He presided over an unprecedented level of giving to Southern Baptist foreign missions. When he joined CBF, that tide continued to flow. By the time he departed the scene toward the twentieth century's end, the young organization was receiving more than $14 million per year, with more than $9 million assigned to global missions. Half of this came in its global missions offering. Ruben Swint, director of the CBF Foundation, noted:

> I have had the privilege of talking with many individuals and couples about their plans to leave a bequest or other estate gift for CBF Global Missions. In nearly every conversation Keith Parks was mentioned by the donors, and they expressed appreciation for Keith's leadership as one of the motivating factors for their gift decision.

Just as much as the money, the personnel flowed in. Through his sermons and personalized invitations to follow Christ into the world, he challenged two generations of young Baptists to respond to unmet needs. He may well have figured personally in the call of more than a thousand missionaries. Some might double that estimate.

Beyond his personal example and his prophetic voice, Parks left to Baptists the timeless principles of missions he had practiced for forty-five years. First was the incarnational principle, or the rule that career missionaries, those who would give their adult lives completely to missions, were the stackpole around which the missions enterprise had to be built. Effective work depended on qualified Baptists who would commit themselves to learning a new language, learning a new culture, and serving as midwives at the birth of indigenous congregations, which would in turn multiply.

The indigeneity held the key to another principle: Don't start institutions for which local people can never assume the costs later. To do so would stymie creativity, mobility, and true partnership. At CBF Parks avoided this in most cases, and the results were a field operating budget majoring on personal ministry and partial project funding, inviting others to pitch in and make a plan work. CBF did not operate as if it had the only water bucket in town to put out the fire.

The last area of his legacy might be categorized as new paradigms. Over and over again, as if to remind himself, too, he declared, "We need to break out of our molds. We need to divorce ourselves from our old habits. We need to be more creative in how people can be involved." From his first or second term on the mission field Parks sought constantly to experiment with new ways of reaching people with the gospel of Jesus. He proved to be the right person in the right place at the right time to institute a revolutionary approach to the last frontiers in missions. He championed the use of the latest computer technology, too, calling it "as high a priority as we have," and thus paved the way for an unprecedented level of communication for far-flung field personnel. This, in turn, played a critical role in the development of self-managed work teams, whose members often found themselves isolated from one another by long distances.

Parks was one of the first to assign missionary teams to people groups rather than countries; he realized that borders were arbitrary barriers that divided peoples and that such peoples needed a unified, multinational approach. In addition, his emphasis on cooperation with other denominations surprised most and delighted many; this indeed was "a new way to be Baptist." His advocacy of the catalytic role, in which missionaries served as facilitators "to make things happen" in world mobilization, prayer coordination, media development, personnel recruitment, and church planting gave World A mission work the critical boost it needed for exponential growth.

This break-the-mold mindset and openness to change gave World A's neglected peoples a champion who could influence a generation of new pioneers. As a result, one of the most important parts of his legacy was the "first fruits" among hundreds of people groups who began hearing the gospel for the first time in their own language, from the Atlas Mountains of North Africa to the arid steppes of Central Asia. According to John Tyler, the Fellowship's moderator for 1998–1999,

> Keith Parks was the right person at the right time for CBF. He came with a vision of what it takes to be faithful and effective in the 1990s, and he knew how to implement that vision. No other person could have come to a fledgling organization and built so quickly an effective global missions program.

The Fellowship has a bright future in global missions simply because Dr. Parks was here to build a solid foundation for us. Ten years from now we'll look at where we are and how far we've come, and then we'll be able to really comprehend what Dr. Parks has meant to us.

At the century's end the popular trend is to note the local church's "taking back" missions responsibility from missionary societies and denominational agencies. Parks understood that trend, but he thought the finest local church "can't do it alone." The local body of believers would always need an agency to help, he contended. This fit the judgment of British missiologist/researcher Patrick Johnstone, who also accepted in the 1990s the local church's retrieval of its original role in missions. Despite this healthy movement, Johnstone argued for retention of a mechanism or channel such as a missions agency in partnership with the local church. Johnstone is widely known as editor of Operation World, a popular, country-by-country handbook for intercessory prayer on world evangelization.

Beyond CBF and, earlier, the Southern Baptist Convention, other Baptists and missions-minded Christians of all denominations should be able to see the same: Keith Parks, above all else, helped lay the foundation for twenty-first-century missions on the last frontiers. Almost anywhere in the world today, if a man or woman, young or old, is searching for more light from God, he or she can find it much more easily, thanks in part to Keith Parks' empowerment of World A pioneers, who in turn facilitated the involvement of many missionary societies, denominations, and parachurch organizations. A seeker will not have to travel quite so far to find a believer and to hear or to read the Scriptures in the "heart language" or mother tongue.

Parks became that solitary seeker's champion, the one who steadfastly advocated for that need. When most everyone else wanted to stop along the way to World A and to address some need closer at hand, Parks tried to turn their eyes once again toward the silent, neglected peoples in parts of Asia and North Africa. He expects to see them in heaven, from every tribe and tongue (Rev 7:9), including sons and daughters of those Kurdish guerillas at the Syrian-Iraqi border who once helped him cross that ancient river.

Keith Parks shares with children at the CBF Chamblee-Doraville (GA) Ministry Center.

Glossary

CBF—Cooperative Baptist Fellowship, the moderate Baptist group formed in the early 1990s in reaction to the fundamentalist takeover of the Southern Baptist Convention. Its headquarters are in Atlanta, Georgia. By late 1998 more than 1,700 churches and many thousands of individuals supported the young movement, with an annual budget of $14 million, $9 million of it for global missions.

CSI—Cooperative Services International, a now-defunct department within the Southern Baptist Foreign Mission Board (now International Mission Board). First formed to send English teachers to China, the department then took responsibility for the new NRM program and eventually became an administrative area similar to regional management of traditional missionary work. By the time of its dismantling in 1997, it had grown to become the largest overseas organism. Parks' successor at the FMB, Jerry Rankin, placed ex-CSI personnel back in the traditional, regional structures. Some top CSI administrators and several missionary families resigned in the aftermath.

Envoy—A Christian on mission who is employed by a corporation or institution but who seeks to engage in the missionary task, joining teams of career missionary personnel in a given locale.

ESL—English as a Second Language, the marketable teaching skill used by many to gain visas from governments hostile to missionary presence and to meet felt needs in other parts of the world.

Ethnolinguistic Clusters—Designations for people groups who have similar cultures and languages.

FMB—Foreign Mission Board, the name for the Southern Baptist Convention's agency for more than 150 years, before being changed to International Mission Board.

GCC—Great Commission Christian, the term used to describe evangelical groups with whom Baptists cooperated in World A.

GMMG—Global Missions Ministry Group, the CBF Coordinating Council's committee charged with overseeing CBF's global missions program, functioning in ways similar to a board of directors or trustees.

GMO—Global Missions Office of CBF.

GSC—Global Service Corps, CBF's personnel category for those serving more than one month and up to two years (with a possible extention of a third year). In 1998 they began bringing, or raising, their own support for service alongside long-term, career missionaries.

GSG—Global Strategy Group, the think tank of Parks' second reorganization at the Foreign Mission Board. Its task was to seek innovative new strategies for responding quickly to needs around the world. Meeting in almost a war-room atmosphere, Parks and his vice presidents tried to break out of their old paradigms, with mixed success.

IBTS—International Baptist Theological Seminary, the European pastors' training school in Prague, Czech Republic. It was moved in 1996 from Ruschlikon, Switzerland, the location famous now among Southern Baptists because of the fundamentalists' decision to "defund" the school in 1991, breaking a promise to provide financial support.

IMB—International Mission Board—The new 1990s name for the Southern Baptist Convention agency formerly known as the Foreign Mission Board.

NAMB—North American Mission Board—The new 1990s name for the Southern Baptist Convention agency formerly known as the Home Mission Board.

NRM—Nonresidential Missionary—The first term used for World A missionaries who focused on a people group in a restricted-access country, such as Saudi Arabia or Iran. This term was later changed to Strategy Coordinator, since creative-access strategies often succeeded in gaining residence in such countries for NRMs.

People Groups—Ethnic populations possessing a common language and culture, often in the minority in a given country or divided by colonial border designations. Their language and culture frequently receive little formal recognition in schools or textbooks.

SC—Strategy Coordinator—The term used for a missionary whose main assignment is to use all good means to assure that a people group has opportunity to hear the Good News of Jesus in their own language and in cultural forms with which they can best identify. Formerly called NRMs, these missionaries serve as advocates, organizers, facilitators catalysts, recruiters and coaches for interdenominational, cooperative efforts.

10-40 Window—A term used to designate the geographical region in a rectangular box between ten and forty degrees latitude across North Africa and Central Asia. Most of the least-evangelized peoples reside in this general area.

Unevangelized Peoples—Those ethnic groups having had little or no opportunity to hear the Good News of Jesus in their own language or cultural forms. Most are found in predominantly Muslim, Hindu, and Buddhist nations of North Africa and Asia.

UPG—Unreached People Group—An ethnic group not having sufficient numbers of churches or Christians among them to assure that all hear the Good News of Jesus without the help of cross-cultural missionaries.

Volunteers—Church members who served on the mission field for one month or less for a specific purpose requested by long-term field personnel.

World A—A Baptist term used to describe roughly one-fifth of the world still awaiting the gospel.

World B— A Baptist term used to describe almost half of the world, those who have heard the gospel but have not responded.

World C—A Baptist term used to describe roughly one-third of the world who have become at least nominally Christian and who share the message with Worlds A and B.